CW00430473

EVERYONE CAN COOK VEGAN

Recipes to celebrate food, save lives and protect our planet

By Maryanne Hall

Viva!

CONTENTS

ABOUT THE AUTHOR

Maryanne is Viva!'s Food & Cookery Manager. In a previous life she was a psychology and history of ideas student, project manager for a European Commission initiative and teacher of English overseas. She first went vegetarian in her teens, before becoming vegan, and since then has been on a non-stop mission to create plant-based dishes which are simple, delicious and indulgent.

Not content with merely cooking as a hobby, Maryanne turned her passion for vegan food into a career. From cheffing in ski chalets, on yoga retreats and at The Green Rocket restaurant in Bath, to running The Health Hub café in Bristol and assisting at Demuths Cookery School, she will be the first to admit she has got about a bit during her career!

Her love of travel, great-tasting food and simplicity has culminated in a recipe book that combines accessibility and ease while, most importantly, never compromising on flavour. Within the pages of this cookbook, you'll find an array of international dishes, the tried-and-tested classics – veganised – healthy protein-rich dishes and mouth-watering treats. All of which are flavour balanced with great texture. You'll find every plant-based recipe you could possibly want for an exciting and varied vegan feast each day of the week! Hopefully we've whetted your appetite sufficiently, but don't just take our word for it, try for yourself and see!

Photo by: Wild Fig Photography

Thanks to

Dean Purnell at **realdesignandmedia.com** for his innovative and beautifully creative graphic design.

Niki Webster at **rebelrecipes.com** for her mouth-wateringly fabulous food photography.

Nicholas Hallows (**nicholashallows@gmail.com**) for his index-writing prowess.

Faye Lewis, Jess Nagji-Nunn, Juliet Gellatley, Justine Butler, Nicholas Hallows and Peter Stillman (**petetheproof@gmail.com**) for their meticulous proofreading skills.

The Viva! team for their absolute dedication to tasting all the recipes and providing invaluable feedback.

Juliet Gellatley for her unwavering support and encouragement.

Front cover photo by Niki Webster at **rebelrecipes.com** of our white chocolate and raspberry cheescake recipe on page 207.

Viva!

INTRODUCTION

We have the utmost faith that this will be the only cookbook you will actually use! After all, we have sourced and collated a mixture of exciting new recipes alongside much-loved classics. But one thing is for certain, they are all delicious, straightforward and seriously indulgent (in the best possible way).

The recipes have been developed for food lovers worldwide who love great taste, but hate fuss. This means our recipes are super accessible when you're craving something delectable but have very little time on your hands. This, of course, goes hand in hand with the Viva! ethos of carrying out campaigning work to save animals, protect the environment, improve our health and help feed the world, because everything in this book is 100 per cent veganlicious!

Whatever your dietary preference, this book will have something for you. It's aimed at all levels of cooks, from the beginner, less confident, or even downright terrible, to the more kitchen savvy amongst you. There are serving suggestions and tips throughout the book, providing inspiration and ideas for jazzing up your favourite meals.

Eating a healthy vegan diet

There's so much variety in plant-based foods, it's incredible, but at the end of the day, a diet rich in fruit, vegetables, wholegrain foods, pulses, nuts and seeds is literally the best thing for you and your gut. It's great to eat locally, seasonally and organically wherever possible. With a vegan diet, you won't be missing out on anything – in fact, much of what you already eat is probably plant-based. With some simple swaps, you can enjoy a wide range of classic dishes plus new and exciting ones.

That said, we understand it's a battle nowadays to eat well all the time. We are being force-fed adverts for terrible ultra-processed foods, and the thing is, we all love them and enjoy them, and to pretend we don't is just nonsense.

So, with that in mind, we've added recipes for some occasional treats, from cakes to meat alternatives that might be unhealthy or highly processed, for eating in moderation. Now pass the chocolate mousse, we mean broccoli!

A word about gluten-free and coeliac dietary requirements

Nearly all of the recipes in the book can easily be adapted for gluten-free and coeliac dietary requirements. Switch out or at least check the label on alcoholic drinks, biscuits, breadcrumbs, bread, cereal, condiments, flour, grains, marinated tofu, noodles, oats, pasta, pesto, plant milk, raising agents (baking powder and bicarbonate of soda), ready-to-roll pastry, soy sauce, stock cubes, vegan dairy alternatives, vegan meat alternatives and yeast extract for gluten-free and coeliac versions. Most major supermarkets, health food shops and online stores now have a wide range of options.

A word about sugar and syrups

You'll find that we've used a bit of sugar or syrup throughout the book for flavour balancing or for our favourite vegan cakes and treats. Feel free to leave these out or substitute them for your best-loved (healthy) sweeteners.

About Viva!

Viva! has been at the forefront of the vegan revolution for three decades. We are the UK's leading vegan campaigning charity. Our dedicated team investigates and campaigns on the impact of diet on animals, our health and the planet. We present talks, cookery demos and provide helpful recipe guides, leaflets and merchandise to support people on their journey towards sustainable and healthy diets.
viva.org.uk

About Vegan Recipe Club

Vegan Recipe Club is part of Viva!'s toolkit to make going – and staying – vegan easy, by providing amazing recipes to make your mouth water! Our website and app bring together three decades' worth of wonderful plant-based recipes, tried-and-tested by the Viva! team. Viva! and Vegan Recipe Club have hundreds of thousands of followers on social media and work with international chefs, brands and influencers to promote the endless benefits of eating vegan food.
veganrecipeclub.org.uk

SMOOTHIES, BREAKFAST AND BRUNCH

Very berry smoothie bowl 10

Yummiest green smoothie 13

Vanilla & almond chia pudding 14

Double chocolate overnight oats 17

4-ingredient crêpes 18

Apple & blueberry breakfast muffins 21

Classic French toast 22

Breakfast quesadillas 25

Super-fast scrambled tofu 26

Scrummy pancakes – sweet or savoury 29

Easy vegan fried eggs 30

Vegan cream cheese & smoked salmon bagels 33

Vegan eggs benedict 34

VERY BERRY SMOOTHIE BOWL

LEVEL: EASY | PREP TIME: 5-10 MINUTES | SERVES: 2

We are just in love with this berrytastic bowl of goodness and all the toppings that go with it – sprinkle on a little bit of, well... everything and enjoy a heavenly treat to start the day!

INGREDIENTS

- **1 large ripe banana, peeled and frozen**
- **250ml sweetened or unsweetened plant milk (depending on how sweet you'd like it)**
- **180g frozen berries of your choice**
- **1 tbsp nut butter of your choice (we used almond)**
- **1 tbsp lemon juice**
- **½ tsp vanilla extract**
- **Handful of fresh spinach**
- **1 date, pitted (optional – add this if you'd like it to be a little sweeter)**
- **1 tbsp vegan protein powder (optional)**

Optional toppings: cacao nibs, chia seeds, chopped dates, chopped nuts, desiccated coconut or coconut flakes, dried fruit, drizzle extra nut butter (if runny), edible flowers, flaxseed, freeze-dried berries, fresh berries, fresh fruit, fresh mint, goji berries, granola, lemon zest, maple syrup, mixed seeds (hemp, sunflower, pumpkin), muesli, nutmeg, pinch of cayenne pepper, cinnamon, sliced banana, vegan chocolate

INSTRUCTIONS

1. Place all the ingredients into a high-speed blender and blend until smooth.
2. Arrange any of the toppings you fancy in a nice pattern and serve immediately.

YUMMIEST GREEN SMOOTHIE

LEVEL: EASY | PREP TIME: 5 MINUTES | SERVES: 1

OK, OK green smoothie – you're probably thinking health hit sure, but flavour urgh!
Well, we're very pleased to tell you that this one tastes like a dessert in a bottle
with a zingy whizz of energy thrown in – we can't get enough!

TIP
—

It's good to have a stash
of ripe frozen bananas in
the freezer for smoothies,
smoothie bowls and
'nice' cream.

INGREDIENTS

- 1½ ripe bananas, peeled and frozen
- Thumbnail of ginger, peeled
- Juice of ½ a lemon
- ½ apple, core and stalk removed
- Handful of spinach or kale leaves, big stalks removed
- 180ml unsweetened plant milk
- 1 tbsp vegan protein powder (optional)
- 70g frozen peas (optional)
- 1 tbsp ground flaxseed (optional)

INSTRUCTIONS

1. Place all the ingredients in a high-speed blender and blend until smooth.
2. Add a little more plant milk if needed or until you reach your desired consistency (especially if using the optional extras).

VANILLA & ALMOND CHIA PUDDING

LEVEL: EASY | PREP TIME: 5 MINUTES | CHILL TIME: 1 HOUR | SERVES: 1

This tiny little seed truly is a nutritional powerhouse – it's an excellent source of energy, healthy omega-3 fats, protein, fibre, calcium, potassium, magnesium, selenium and iron – wow, we're sold! Add creamy nut butter, vanilla and syrup and you've got one seriously tasty brekkie!

INGREDIENTS

- 125ml unsweetened plant milk
- 1 tbsp nut butter
- 1 tbsp syrup (eg maple or agave)
- 1 tsp vanilla extract
- Pinch of salt
- 2 tbsp chia seeds

Optional toppings: berries, berry compote, cacao nibs, chopped nuts, coconut flakes, drizzle extra nut butter (if runny), extra syrup, fresh fruit, granola, jam, peanuts, sliced bananas, vegan caramel sauce, vegan chocolate

INSTRUCTIONS

1. Using a high-speed blender, blend the plant milk, nut butter, syrup, vanilla and salt until smooth.
2. Pour into a glass or container with a lid (if transporting) then stir through the chia seeds until thoroughly combined. Leave it to sit for 5 minutes.
3. Give it another good stir then place in the fridge for a minimum of an hour.
4. Stir the pudding again, add the toppings of your choice and enjoy.

DOUBLE CHOCOLATE OVERNIGHT OATS

LEVEL: EASY | PREP TIME: 5 MINUTES PLUS OVERNIGHT SOAKING TIME | SERVES: 1

Bounce out of bed for a mouth-watering, super-fuelled start to the day! Quickly prep these indulgent oats the night before, ready to grab and go the next morning!

INGREDIENTS

- 50g rolled oats
- 180ml unsweetened plant milk
- ½ tsp vanilla extract
- 1 tbsp nut or seed butter of your choice
- 2 tsp chia seeds
- 1-2 tbsp (depending on how chocolatey you like it) raw cacao or cocoa powder
- 1 tbsp syrup (eg maple or agave)
- 2 tbsp vegan dark chocolate chips or cacao nibs
- Pinch of salt

Optional toppings: berries or any other chopped fruit you fancy, cinnamon, coconut flakes, desiccated coconut, dried fruit, fresh mint, granola, hemp seeds, jam, mixed nuts, muesli, nut butter, pumpkin seeds, sliced banana, sunflower seeds, vegan chocolate sauce or melted chocolate, vegan yoghurt

INSTRUCTIONS

1. Using a small mason jar or small airtight bowl/box, add all the ingredients and stir until thoroughly combined.
2. Add any of the toppings you like or you can add them the next day if preferred.
3. Leave overnight in the fridge ready to grab and go the next morning!

4-INGREDIENT CRÊPES

LEVEL: EASY | PREP TIME: 2 MINUTES | COOK TIME: 10 MINUTES | SERVES: 6

Eat a Parisian breakfast in the comfort of your own home. The crêpe batter is incredibly simple to make and then you just get to have fun with the fillings!

INGREDIENTS

- 150g plain flour
- ¼ tsp salt
- 350ml unsweetened plant milk
- 1 tbsp neutral oil (eg rapeseed), plus extra for frying

INSTRUCTIONS

1. In a large bowl, mix the flour and salt together before stirring in the plant milk and oil.
2. Heat a little oil in a crêpe pan or wide, non-stick frying pan on a medium-high heat.
3. When the oil is hot, pour a small ladle of batter into the pan, swirling it around so that it thinly coats the pan.
4. Fry on both sides until lightly golden.

SAVOURY SERVING SUGGESTIONS
—

Balsamic glaze, capers, fried leeks, fried mushrooms, garlic mushrooms, green pesto, maple syrup, mustard dressing, olives, tomatoes, vegan bacon, vegan blue cheese, vegan cheese, vegan chicken pieces, vegan cream cheese, vegan feta, vegan garlic sauce/mayonnaise, vegan ham, vegan plain yoghurt, vegan salmon, vegan sausage slices, wilted spinach

SWEET SERVING SUGGESTIONS
—

Caramelised apples, chopped pistachios, cinnamon, coconut flakes, cooked cinnamon apples, flaked almonds, fresh berries, fresh fruit, grated coconut, lemon juice, maple syrup, mixed nuts, nut butter, sliced banana, strawberries, strawberry sauce, sugar, vegan butter, vegan caramel sauce, vegan chocolate sauce, vegan chocolate spread, vegan cream (double or squirty), vegan ice cream, vegan marshmallows

APPLE & BLUEBERRY BREAKFAST MUFFINS

LEVEL: EASY | PREP TIME: 10 MINUTES | COOK TIME: 30 MINUTES | SERVES: 8-10

Created by Viva!'s Helen Wilson, former Food and Cookery Coordinator, these muffins have got all the essentials for a delicious and unexpectedly hearty breakfast on the go. They contain oats for energy, nut butter for protein and fruit for a zingy vitamin hit. Make up a batch then freeze them or eat them up throughout the week. They'll stay fresh for up to 4 days in an airtight container.

INGREDIENTS

- 150g muesli
- 100g light brown sugar
- 160g plain flour
- 1 tsp baking powder
- 1 tsp ground cinnamon
- Pinch of salt
- 150g blueberries
- 250ml sweetened plant milk
- 1 apple, peeled and grated
- 2 tbsp vegetable oil
- 3 tbsp nut butter
- 20g raisins or sultanas
- Handful of sunflower seeds (optional)
- Syrup (eg maple or agave) for drizzling (optional)

INSTRUCTIONS

1. Preheat the oven to 180°C/350°F/Gas Mark 4.
2. Line a muffin tin with 8 paper muffin cases.
3. In a large bowl, combine the muesli with the sugar, flour, baking powder, cinnamon, salt and blueberries (don't squish them – keep them whole).
4. In a jug, thoroughly mix the plant milk, apple, oil, nut butter and raisins/sultanas.
5. Stir this liquid mix into the dry ingredients with a wooden spoon.
6. Once combined, divide the mixture equally between the muffin cases until about three-quarters full. Sprinkle over the sunflower seeds if using.
7. Bake for 25-30 minutes or until the muffins are risen and golden.
8. Drizzle over some syrup (if using) and enjoy.

CLASSIC FRENCH TOAST

LEVEL: EASY | PREP TIME: 5 MINUTES | COOK TIME: 10 MINUTES | SERVES: 2-3

Fun fact: French toast is known in France as 'pain perdu' which means 'lost bread' – referring to this dish's amazing ability to rescue stale bread and turn it into something delicious! Every non-vegan who has ever tried this vegan eggy bread has been blown away by how authentic it tastes! The great thing about this recipe is that it can be turned into a sweet or savoury dish (the batter is the same for both) so enjoy getting creative!

INGREDIENTS

- 175g silken tofu (ideally firm silken tofu)
- 120ml unsweetened plant milk
- 1 tbsp vegetable oil
- 1 tbsp nutritional yeast
- ¾ tsp salt (use Kala Namak/black salt to create 'eggy' taste)
- Pinch of black pepper
- 4-6 slices of bread, medium thick

INSTRUCTIONS

1. Using a high-speed blender, blend all the ingredients together, apart from the bread, until very smooth.
2. Heat a non-stick frying pan until hot then add a little oil, covering the bottom of the pan.
3. Depending on the size of your frying pan, coat 1-2 slices of bread in the mixture and place in the pan.
4. Cook for several minutes on each side until quite crispy and golden brown – make sure the bread isn't soggy.
5. Repeat the process until the mixture is used up. Serve hot.

SWEET SERVING SUGGESTIONS
—
Chopped banana, chopped nuts, coconut flakes, fresh berries, ground cinnamon, maple syrup, nut butter, plain vegan yoghurt, vegan chocolate spread

SAVOURY SERVING SUGGESTIONS
—
Avocado, cherry tomatoes, full vegan breakfast, maple syrup, vegan bacon, vegan cheese, vegan ham, vegan sausages, wilted spinach

BREAKFAST QUESADILLAS

LEVEL: EASY | PREP TIME: 10 MINUTES | COOK TIME: 5 MINUTES | SERVES: 1-2

We'll let you into a secret: this dish can actually be made for breakfast, brunch, lunch or dinner! This Mexican treat involves sandwiching lashings of melted vegan cheese together with tomatoes, black beans, greens and spices. We think you'll be surprised by how straightforward it is and it really sets you up for the day. Created by Jane Easton, Viva!'s former Food and Cookery Manager and all-round foodie star.

INGREDIENTS

QUESADILLAS
- ½ tin black beans, drained and rinsed
- 2 medium tomatoes, roughly chopped
- 2 tbsp tomato sauce or purée
- 1 spring onion, finely chopped
- ½ tsp salt
- Pinch of black pepper
- 1 tsp smoked paprika
- Large handful of vegan cheese, grated
- 2 large wraps or corn tortillas

QUICK GUACAMOLE
- 1 large ripe avocado, mashed then placed in a bowl
- 1 clove garlic, crushed
- 1 tbsp lime or lemon juice
- Pinch of salt and pepper
- ¼ red onion, finely diced (optional)
- ½ ripe tomato, finely diced (optional)
- Pinch of chilli powder or hot pepper sauce (optional)
- Small handful of fresh coriander, stalks removed (optional)

INSTRUCTIONS

QUESADILLAS
1. Mash the black beans roughly. Add the tomatoes, tomato sauce or purée, spring onion, salt, pepper and smoked paprika.
2. Spread the mixture on one of the wraps then sprinkle with the vegan cheese. Place the other wrap over the top.
3. Either fry the quesadilla on both sides until lightly golden (be careful when flipping that the filling doesn't spill out), warm each side under a hot grill or pop it in the microwave for a minute.
4. Cut into quarters and serve warm.

QUICK GUACAMOLE
1. Add all the ingredients to the bowl of avocado and thoroughly combine.

SUPER-FAST SCRAMBLED TOFU

LEVEL: EASY | PREP TIME: 5 MINUTES | COOK TIME: 5 MINUTES | SERVES: 1-2

This dish is an absolute must-have in your weekly assortment of recipes! It only takes 10 minutes to make, it's high in protein, really delicious and can be eaten for breakfast, lunch or dinner.

INGREDIENTS

- 1 clove garlic, finely chopped
- 175g firm tofu, drained and patted dry or use firm or regular silken tofu, gently broken up into bite-sized pieces
- 1 tsp tahini
- 1 tbsp soy sauce
- 1 tbsp nutritional yeast
- ½ tsp turmeric
- Splash of unsweetened plant milk (optional)
- Pinch of salt and pepper (optional)

Optional extras: alfalfa sprouts, lightly cooked cherry tomatoes, mixed seeds, sliced avocado, wilted spinach

INSTRUCTIONS

1. Gently fry the garlic in a little oil in a small saucepan or frying pan on a medium heat for about 30 seconds until lightly golden. Don't let it burn.
2. Add all the other ingredients to the pan and mix together.
3. If you would like the mixture to be a little less dry then gradually add a splash of plant milk until you achieve your desired consistency.
4. Heat for approximately 3-5 minutes to warm through and serve immediately.
5. Taste and add more soy sauce, nutritional yeast and tahini, if needed.

SERVING SUGGESTIONS
—

Avocado, baked beans, barbecue sauce, breakfast muffins, cooked tomatoes, fresh herbs, fried potatoes, grilled asparagus, grilled or fried mushrooms, hash browns, pancakes, roasted or steamed vegetables, salad, shakshuka, toast, vegan bacon, vegan sausages, wraps

SCRUMMY PANCAKES - SWEET OR SAVOURY

LEVEL: EASY | PREP TIME: 5 MINUTES | COOK TIME: 10 MINUTES | SERVES: 4

The thing we like best about these pancakes is that you just make the simple batter and then dress them up to create a sweet or savoury delight. We've featured a tasty savoury treat (see photo) but we also love a good helping of vegan chocolate spread with fresh berries and a dusting of icing sugar – yum! Makes 8 pancakes.

INGREDIENTS

DRY INGREDIENTS
- **350g plain flour (you can use half plain, half wholemeal flour for a healthier version)**
- **4 tbsp gram/chickpea flour, sieved**
- **2 tsp baking powder**
- **¼ tsp salt**

WET INGREDIENTS
- **350ml unsweetened plant milk**
- **350ml water**
- **2 tbsp vegetable oil**

INSTRUCTIONS

1. Place all the ingredients in a blender and blend until smooth. Alternatively, whisk by hand until there are no lumps. If hand whisking, thoroughly combine the dry ingredients first then add the wet ingredients gradually.
2. Heat a non-stick frying pan on a medium heat and then add a small amount of oil (a hot pan makes better pancakes).
3. Pour enough of the batter mixture into the frying pan to thinly cover the bottom. Fry on one side for about a minute. Loosen the edges with a spatula and flip. Fry the flip side for another minute or until cooked through and lightly golden.
4. Remove from pan and keep warm in the oven on its lowest setting.
5. Add more oil to the pan if and when necessary. Repeat steps 3 and 4 until all of the mixture is used up.

SWEET SERVING SUGGESTIONS

—

Caramelised apple, fresh berries, lemon juice, maple syrup, sliced banana, sugar, vegan chocolate spread, vegan ice cream, vegan yoghurt

SAVOURY SERVING SUGGESTIONS

—

Avocado, fried cherry tomatoes, fried potatoes, garlic mushrooms, scrambled tofu, vegan cheese, vegan ham, vegan lardons or vegan bacon, vegan mayonnaise, vegan tuna, wilted spinach

EASY VEGAN FRIED EGGS

LEVEL: EASY | PREP TIME: 10 MINUTES | COOK TIME: 15 MINUTES | SERVES: 4

We just love how realistic these vegan fried eggs are – and how easy they are to make too! Delight friends and family and have fun in the process, without the cholesterol of course! The recipe will make around 8 vegan fried eggs. Use any leftover yolk for dipping soldiers.

INGREDIENTS

YOLKS
- 200g carrots, squash or pumpkin, peeled and sliced or cut into 2cm cubes
- 1 tbsp olive oil plus extra for frying
- 2 tbsp nutritional yeast
- 2 tbsp cornflour
- 1 tbsp unsweetened plant milk
- ½ tsp black salt (Kala Namak)
- ⅛ tsp regular salt
- ⅛ tsp turmeric

WHITES
- 140ml unsweetened plant milk
- 90g rice flour
- ½ tsp salt
- 1 tbsp water
- 1 tbsp olive oil

SERVING SUGGESTIONS
—
Avocado, barbecue sauce, breakfast muffins, brown sauce, dirty fries, fried rice, full vegan breakfast, grilled tomatoes, nasi goreng, rocket, shakshuka, toasted bagels, toast with vegan butter, wilted spinach

INSTRUCTIONS

YOLKS
1. Boil or steam the butternut squash, carrots or pumpkin until soft. Thoroughly drain any excess water.
2. Place the steamed vegetables along with all the other yolk ingredients into a high-speed blender and blend until very smooth. The consistency needs to be thick and gloopy. Set aside until needed.

WHITES
1. Using a medium-sized bowl, whisk all the ingredients together until very smooth. Set aside until needed.

COOKING
1. Using a large non-stick frying pan (with a lid), heat a little oil on medium then add 2 tablespoons of the egg white mixture. Fry for around 30 seconds.
2. Place 1 level tablespoon of the yolk mixture neatly into the centre of the white. Place the lid on and then cook for 2-3 minutes but don't flip. Remove with a spatula and cook the rest of the eggs using the same method (you might need to add a little more oil to the pan).
3. After you've mastered the technique, you can try cooking multiple eggs at the same time.

VEGAN CREAM CHEESE & SMOKED SALMON BAGELS

SERVING SUGGESTIONS

—

Cucumber salad, fresh or grilled tomatoes, lemon wedges, salads

**LEVEL: EASY | PREP TIME: 10 MINUTES | COOK TIME: 5 MINUTES
MARINATING TIME: 2 HOURS OR OVERNIGHT | SERVES: 4**

You won't quite believe how realistic this is – and using carrots! Don't take our word for it – try it for yourselves…

INGREDIENTS

VEGAN SMOKED SALMON
- **3 large carrots, peeled then sliced into thick ribbons using a vegetable peeler**

MARINADE
- **1 tsp white miso paste**
- **4 tbsp neutral oil (eg rapeseed)**
- **¼ tsp salt**
- **2 tsp syrup (eg maple or agave)**
- **1 tsp smoked paprika**
- **1 tbsp lemon juice**
- **1 nori sheet, cut into 4 strips or 1 tsp nori flakes**

OTHER INGREDIENTS
- **4 plain bagels, halved, toasted and spread with vegan butter**
- **Vegan plain cream cheese (use approx. 3 tbsp per whole bagel/ serving)**

Optional toppings: capers, cucumber ribbons, finely sliced onion rings, fresh dill, sliced avocado, sliced spring onion, vegan crème fraîche

INSTRUCTIONS

VEGAN SMOKED SALMON

1. Steam the carrot ribbons for about 5 minutes. Check them after 3-4 minutes because you don't want them to get soggy! They need to be very lightly cooked. Let the carrots cool a little bit but still keep them warm.

MARINADE

1. Using a medium-sized bowl, stir all the ingredients together thoroughly.

2. Place the warm (ish) carrot ribbons into the marinade and mix well without mashing up the carrot.

3. Pop the carrot and the marinade in an airtight container and leave to absorb the flavours for a minimum of 2 hours.

4. If using nori sheets, remove them before serving.

OTHER INGREDIENTS

1. Spread the vegan cream cheese onto the freshly toasted bagels and arrange the vegan smoked salmon evenly over each of them.

VEGAN EGGS BENEDICT

LEVEL: NOT TOO TRICKY | PREP TIME: 20 MINUTES | COOK TIME: 5-10 MINUTES | SERVES: 2

Enjoy a veganised crispy tofu version of this classic brunch! The black salt creates a perfectly 'eggy' taste and the creamy hollandaise finishes off the dish delightfully.

INGREDIENTS

HOLLANDAISE SAUCE
- 150ml unsweetened soya milk (needs to be soya milk for this one)
- 1 tbsp cider vinegar or white wine vinegar
- 1 tsp Dijon mustard
- ½ tsp black salt (Kala Namak)
- ½ tsp garlic powder
- ¼ tsp turmeric
- ¼ tsp cayenne pepper
- 1 tbsp lemon juice
- 1 tsp syrup (eg maple or agave)
- 150ml neutral oil (eg rapeseed)

TOFU COATING
- 50g nutritional yeast
- 30g cornflour
- 1 tsp garlic powder
- Pinch of salt and pepper

TOFU
- 225g (approx.) extra firm tofu, cut into 2cm thick slices
- 4 tbsp soy sauce
- 1 tbsp rapeseed oil

MUFFINS
- 2 English breakfast muffins, halved, toasted and spread with vegan butter

Optional toppings: chilli sauce, chopped chives or parsley

INSTRUCTIONS

HOLLANDAISE SAUCE
1. Add all the ingredients (apart from the oil) to a large jug.
2. Using a stick blender, blend all the ingredients together, adding the oil a little bit at a time until the mixture becomes thick and creamy. Set aside.

TOFU COATING
1. Mix all the ingredients together in a bowl and set aside.

TOFU
1. Whisk the soy sauce and rapeseed oil together in a bowl and set aside.
2. Fully immerse the tofu slices in the soy sauce/oil mix then immediately dip them in the tofu coating. Make sure that each slice is fully coated then press down to make sure it sticks properly.
3. Fry the fully coated tofu slices in a little oil, on both sides, until golden.

ASSEMBLY
1. In a small saucepan, gently warm the hollandaise sauce on a low-medium heat.
2. Place the tofu slices on top of the toasted breakfast muffins, along with any of the optional serving suggestions.
3. Pour the warmed hollandaise sauce over the top and serve.

SERVING SUGGESTIONS
—
Fried cherry tomatoes, fried potatoes, garlic mushrooms, grilled asparagus, sliced avocado, vegan bacon, wilted spinach

SALADS AND SANDWICHES

Creamy tahini kale salad 38

Chickless Caesar salad 41

White bean, olive & cherry tomato salad with vegan feta 42

Warm Moroccan salad with spicy harissa drizzle 45

Coronation vegan chicken (or chickpea) sandwich 46

Tofu banh mi 49

Italian tempeh open sandwich with balsamic glaze 50

Vegan egg & cress baguette 53

CREAMY TAHINI KALE SALAD

LEVEL: EASY | PREP TIME: 5 MINUTES | SERVES: 1-2

Juliet, Founder and International Director of Viva!, was not a fan of kale salad and was unsure about including this recipe in the cookbook. Of course, we accepted the challenge, made her a deliciously large helping and waited – she came out of her office declaring it was one of the best salads she'd ever eaten! We'd love for you to find out for yourselves...

INGREDIENTS

SALAD
- **Big bunch of kale, stalks removed and torn into bite-sized pieces**

DRESSING
- **3 tbsp olive oil**
- **3 tbsp tahini**
- **3 tbsp cider vinegar**
- **2 tbsp soy sauce**
- **1 tbsp syrup (eg maple or agave)**

Optional extras: any tinned pulses (drained and rinsed), artichokes, avocado, cherry tomatoes, croutons, cucumber, fresh chilli, fresh herbs, garlic, grated beetroot, marinated tofu, quinoa, radish, red onion, spring onion, sprinkling of nutritional yeast, sundried tomatoes, sweetcorn, toasted mixed seeds (see page 176)

INSTRUCTIONS

1. Place the torn kale into a large bowl and pour over all the dressing ingredients.
2. Massage the dressing ingredients into the kale leaves for a good couple of minutes (this helps to break down the fibres in the kale to make it more digestible and also helps it to absorb the flavours!).
3. Add any of the optional extras of your choice (and more of the dressing ingredients if needed) and enjoy!

SERVING SUGGESTIONS
—

Bulgur wheat, couscous, crusty bread, curries, pasta or gnocchi, quinoa, rice and tofu, roasted vegetables, selection of salads, vegan kiev

CHICKLESS CAESAR SALAD

LEVEL: EASY | PREP TIME: 10 MINUTES | COOK TIME: 5-10 MINUTES | SERVES: 4

Consistently one of the most popular salads on the Vegan Recipe Club due to its simplicity and tastiness. Caesar salad doesn't need much of an introduction, so we'll stop chatting and let you get prepping!

INGREDIENTS

SALAD
- **350g (approx.) vegan chicken strips/pieces or make 1 batch of either tofu recipe on page 140**
- **2 baby gem or 1 cos or romaine lettuce, leaves separated**
- **1 avocado, sliced**
- **200g cherry tomatoes, halved**
- **2 handfuls of croutons (we made our own using 2cm squares of sourdough bread, crusts removed, drizzled with a little oil and salt and placed in the oven at 180°C/350°F/Gas Mark 4 until golden)**
- **Handful of fresh parsley, stalks removed and finely chopped**
- **50g vegan Parmesan, shaved or grated (or buy a pre-grated version and sprinkle over)**
- **1 tbsp capers, drained and rinsed (optional)**

DRESSING
- **230g vegan mayonnaise**
- **1 tsp Dijon mustard**
- **2 cloves garlic, crushed**
- **2 tbsp lemon juice**
- **50g vegan Parmesan, grated (or buy a pre-grated version)**
- **¼ tsp salt**
- **¼ tsp black pepper**
- **1 tsp vegan Worcestershire sauce (optional)**

INSTRUCTIONS

SALAD
1. Lightly fry the vegan chicken pieces in a little oil until golden or according to the instructions on the packet.
2. Arrange all the different salad ingredients together in a bowl.

DRESSING
1. Mix all the ingredients together in a medium-sized bowl until well combined.
2. Either spoon a few dollops of the dressing over the salad ingredients or mix together with the salad until fully covered.

WHITE BEAN, OLIVE & CHERRY TOMATO SALAD WITH VEGAN FETA

LEVEL: EASY | PREP TIME: 10 MINUTES | SERVES: 4 AS A SIDE DISH

Add some grains to create a hearty main meal or enjoy as a delicious accompaniment to a variety of dishes!

INGREDIENTS

SALAD

- 1 x 400g tin white beans (eg cannellini or butter beans), drained and rinsed
- 300g (approx.) cherry tomatoes, halved
- Handful of olives
- 1 clove garlic, finely chopped
- Handful of fresh parsley, stalks removed and roughly chopped
- 100g (approx.) vegan feta or vegan Greek-style cheese (or use the tofu salad pieces recipe below)
- Salt and pepper, to taste

DRESSING

- 2 tbsp olive oil
- 2 tbsp lemon juice
- 1 tbsp red wine vinegar (use this ideally but if you don't have any, cider vinegar is OK)
- 1 tsp syrup (eg maple or agave)
- Pinch of salt and pepper

TOFU SALAD PIECES

- 200g tofu, drained, patted dry, cut into 2cm cubes and set aside
- 2 tbsp white miso paste
- 2 tbsp cider vinegar
- 2 tbsp lemon juice
- 3 tbsp olive oil
- 2 tsp syrup (eg maple or agave)
- 2 cloves garlic, crushed
- 1½ tbsp nutritional yeast
- ¼ tsp onion powder
- ½ tsp salt
- ¼ tsp black pepper
- ¼ tsp chilli flakes
- 2 tsp dried oregano

INSTRUCTIONS

SALAD

1. In a large bowl gently mix all the ingredients together and add salt and pepper to your taste.

DRESSING

1. Whisk all the ingredients together in a bowl, then drizzle over the salad and stir through.

TOFU SALAD PIECES

1. Blend the miso, cider vinegar, lemon juice, olive oil, syrup, garlic, nutritional yeast, onion powder and salt until smooth.
2. Stir through the black pepper, chilli flakes and oregano then pour the dressing over the tofu cubes, making sure they are thoroughly coated. Place in the fridge for a minimum of 30 minutes before eating.
3. Store in an airtight container and use within 3 days.

TIP

—

Use the tofu salad pieces recipe for salads, sandwiches and snacking.

SERVING SUGGESTIONS

—

Barbecues, burgers, crusty bread, Greek dishes, lasagne, picnics, pizza, quiche, salads, sandwiches, summer tarts, tagines, vegan fillets, vegan frittata or farinata, vegan omelette

WARM MOROCCAN SALAD WITH SPICY HARISSA DRIZZLE

LEVEL: EASY | PREP TIME: 10 MINUTES | COOK TIME: 30 MINUTES | SERVES: 4

This protein-packed rainbow feast of a salad is perfect for weekday evenings when there are hungry bellies and little time. Drizzle with our harissa dressing for a smoky, spicy kick – and we really recommend pouring over some tahini sauce too (see page 167) for a little extra indulgence!

INGREDIENTS

HARISSA DRESSING
- 4 tbsp harissa paste (we like rose harissa)
- 6 tbsp olive oil
- 2 tbsp white wine vinegar
- 2 tsp syrup (eg maple or agave) or sugar
- 4 tbsp boiling water

SALAD
- 2 red onions, peeled and quartered
- 2 red or yellow peppers, deseeded and cut into bite-sized chunks
- 2 sweet potatoes, peeled and cut into bite-sized chunks
- 2 large carrots, peeled and sliced into 2cm chunks
- 1 x 400g tin chickpeas, drained and rinsed
- 1-2 tsp cumin seeds
- 200g couscous, giant couscous, quinoa or bulgur wheat, cooked according to the instructions on the packet
- 2 handfuls of raisins, sultanas or chopped apricots (optional)
- 2 handfuls of blanched almonds, flaked almonds, pistachios or walnuts, ideally toasted or roasted (see page 178)
- 100g mixed leaves

Optional toppings: fresh coriander or mint, our delicious tahini sauce (see page 167), pomegranate seeds, vegan plain yoghurt

INSTRUCTIONS

HARISSA DRESSING
1. Stir all the ingredients together in a small jug or mug until thoroughly combined. Set aside.

SALAD
1. Preheat the oven to 200°C/390°F/Gas Mark 6.
2. Evenly space the onions, peppers, sweet potatoes and carrots on a large baking tray. Lightly coat in oil and a sprinkling of salt (you might want to get your hands in there!).
3. Place in the oven for 15 minutes then remove the tray, turn over the vegetables and add the chickpeas and cumin seeds to the tray.
4. Place back into the oven for 15 minutes or until the vegetables are golden and slightly caramelised.
5. In a large bowl, gently combine your chosen grain (eg giant couscous), roasted vegetables, chickpeas, raisins and nuts.
6. On a serving platter arrange the leaves, vegetables and grain mix and then top with the harissa dressing and other optional toppings.

TIP
—
You can use the harissa dressing on a variety of salads, stews, burgers, wraps, Middle Eastern dishes, roasted or steamed vegetables and pasta.

CORONATION VEGAN CHICKEN (OR CHICKPEA) SANDWICH

LEVEL: EASY | PREP TIME: 5 MINUTES | COOK TIME: 5-10 MINUTES | SERVES: 4

As the name suggests, this is a traditional British royal dish but we've jazzed it up and veganised the whole affair! It's equally delicious with vegan chicken or chickpeas but the chickpea option is much quicker as you don't have to cook anything. The sandwich tastes great without the optional extras but if you want to add a bit of extra spice and green bits then go for the full works!

INGREDIENTS

- 250g vegan chicken pieces, lightly fried according to instructions on the packet or 2 x 400g tins chickpeas, drained and rinsed
- 6 tbsp vegan mayonnaise
- 1 tbsp mango chutney or apricot jam
- ¼ tsp ground cinnamon
- 2 tsp mild curry powder
- 2 tbsp raisins, sultanas or chopped dried apricots
- Pinch of salt and black pepper
- Handful of fresh coriander, stalks removed and roughly chopped (optional)
- 2 spring onions, ends removed and finely sliced (optional)
- 1 tsp lemon juice (optional)
- ½ red chilli, deseeded and finely chopped (optional)
- 8 slices bread with vegan butter/spread

INSTRUCTIONS

1. Lightly fry the chicken pieces according to the instructions on the packet then leave to cool for 10 minutes.
2. Stir all the other ingredients together in a bowl (apart from the bread!) and add the vegan chicken once it's ready. If using chickpeas instead, then mash them up a bit.
3. Divide the filling evenly between 4 sandwiches and enjoy.
4. Alternatively, you can keep the filling in an airtight container in the fridge for up to 5 days.

TIP
—

You can also serve this sandwich warm by heating in a frying pan without oil or under the grill.

TOFU BANH MI

LEVEL: NOT TOO TRICKY | PREP TIME: 30 MINUTES | COOK TIME: 10 MINUTES | SERVES: 4

There are lots of ways to cheat with this recipe if you're short of time! You can use marinated tofu or try switching the pickled vegetables for kimchi or pre-pickled daikon. Of course, it's best if you make it in full but an awesome sarnie either way!

INGREDIENTS

TOFU
To save time, buy marinated tofu instead (although it's really worth making your own)

- **450g firm or extra firm tofu, cut into 0.5cm slices**
- **6 tbsp soy sauce**
- **2 tbsp soft brown sugar**
- **Thumbnail of fresh ginger, peeled and finely chopped**
- **Juice of 1 lime**

PICKLED VEGETABLES
To save time, use kimchi, pickled daikon radish or mixed vegetables (fukujinzuke) instead

- **2 small carrots, peeled, halved lengthways and cut into thin sticks**
- **1 turnip, peeled and cut into thin sticks – the same size as the carrot sticks**
- **6 tbsp white wine vinegar**
- **2 tbsp soft brown sugar**
- **½ tsp salt**

TO SERVE
- **4 small baguettes**
- **½ cucumber, deseeded and cut into thin sticks**
- **Spring onions, ends removed and sliced**
- **Handful of fresh coriander, roughly chopped**
- **Handful of fresh mint, stalks removed and roughly chopped**
- **Squeeze of fresh lime juice**
- **Vegan mayonnaise**
- **Sriracha (optional)**

INSTRUCTIONS

TOFU
1. Place the tofu slices on a baking tray in a single layer.
2. Mix the soy sauce, brown sugar, ginger and lime together in a mug. Pour it over the tofu so that it's evenly covered. Ideally leave to marinate for a minimum of 30 minutes, turning the slices once.

PICKLED VEGETABLES
1. While the tofu is marinating, make the pickled vegetables.
2. Place the carrots and turnip in a small bowl and set aside.
3. Using a small saucepan, add the vinegar, sugar and salt.
4. Bring to the boil, making sure the sugar has dissolved, then pour immediately over the sliced vegetables. Make sure they are thoroughly coated then set aside to cool.

TO SERVE
1. Fry the tofu slices on both sides until golden brown.
2. While the tofu is frying, fill each of the baguettes evenly using the filling ingredients, including the pickled vegetables.
3. When the tofu is ready, divide the slices up between the baguettes and add more vegan mayonnaise and sriracha if needed.

ITALIAN TEMPEH OPEN SANDWICH WITH BALSAMIC GLAZE

LEVEL: EASY | PREP TIME: 10 MINUTES | COOK TIME: 10 MINUTES | SERVES: 2

Don't be put off by the length of this recipe because it's incredibly quick and easy! One of the Viva! team said it was the best sandwich they'd ever eaten – oh, and there's no marinating involved, even better!

INGREDIENTS

TEMPEH SAUCE
- 2 tbsp olive oil
- 3 tbsp balsamic vinegar
- 1 tbsp Italian mixed herbs
- 1 tbsp nutritional yeast
- 1 tsp onion powder
- 1 tsp syrup (eg maple or agave)
- ½ tsp salt
- ¼ tsp black pepper

TEMPEH
- 200g tempeh, cut into 0.5cm thick slices (either rectangles, triangles or circles depending on the shape of your tempeh block or preference)
- Sprinkling of salt
- 2 cloves garlic, finely chopped

OTHER
- 2 soft ciabatta rolls (or any bread/rolls of your choice), sliced in half and option to lightly toast
- 2 tbsp vegan green pesto (either use shop-bought or homemade – see page 164)
- 1 tomato, sliced
- Handful of roasted peppers (from a jar), drained
- 1 tbsp capers, drained
- 50g vegan mozzarella (or any vegan cheese of your choice)
- Handful of fresh basil leaves, stalks removed
- Handful of fresh rocket (optional)
- Balsamic glaze (for drizzling)
- Salt and pepper, to taste

INSTRUCTIONS

TEMPEH SAUCE
1. Mix all the ingredients together in a jug or mug and set aside.

TEMPEH
1. Fry the tempeh in a little oil and a sprinkling of salt until golden on both sides, turning once.
2. Add the garlic to the pan and fry for 2 minutes.
3. Pour the tempeh sauce over the tempeh and into the pan. Turn the tempeh pieces over making sure they are covered in the sauce on both sides. Fry for a further 2 minutes.

OTHER/ASSEMBLY
1. Place the rolls sliced side up.
2. Spread the pesto evenly over the open rolls.
3. Evenly distribute the tomato, roasted peppers and capers.
4. Add the tempeh then vegan mozzarella and melt under the grill if you prefer it warm and melted.
5. Finish off the sandwiches with the basil, rocket and a drizzle of balsamic glaze.
6. Add a sprinkling of salt and pepper to your taste.

VEGAN EGG & CRESS BAGUETTE

LEVEL: EASY | PREP TIME: 10 MINUTES | SERVES: 4

Here's a throwback to the first Viva! cookbook, written by Jane Easton! Be the envy of every picnic with this scrumptious (and very easy) classic – you won't know the difference!

INGREDIENTS

VEGAN EGG MIX

- **250g firm tofu, drained, patted dry and crumbled**
- **1 tsp English, Dijon or wholegrain mustard**
- **½ tsp turmeric**
- **½ tsp black salt (Kala Namak)**
- **¼ tsp black pepper**
- **1½ tbsp nutritional yeast**
- **5 tbsp vegan mayonnaise**
- **Handful of cress**
- **½ red onion, finely diced (optional)**
- **2 tsp chives, finely chopped (optional)**

OTHER

- **4 x small baguettes or 8 slices bread, spread with vegan butter**
- **2 tomatoes, sliced (optional)**
- **Handful of lettuce leaves, torn into smaller pieces (optional)**

INSTRUCTIONS

VEGAN EGG MIX

1. In a mixing bowl, stir all the ingredients together until thoroughly combined.

OTHER/ASSEMBLY

1. Divide the vegan egg mix evenly between all of the baguettes or bread slices.

2. Add the tomato and lettuce, if using, and serve.

LUNCHES AND SOUPS

15-minute Thai soup 56

Creamy mushroom soup with sherry & thyme 59

Golden butternut squash & miso soup 60

Toast with all the good stuff 63

DIY pot noodle 64

Cheesy mushroom omelette 67

Crispy potato & tofu rostis with caramelised onion chutney 68

Broccoli & tomato quiche 71

Sushi dragon roll with spicy tahini sauce 72

15-MINUTE THAI SOUP

DIFFICULTY: EASY | PREP TIME: 5 MINUTES | COOK TIME: 10 MINUTES | SERVES: 2

This might just be one of the easiest and fastest soup recipes you've ever made! Packed full of beautiful Thai flavours and fresh vegetables, it's a tasty and nutritious hug in a mug. No more boring lunches!

INGREDIENTS

- 1 large carrot, peeled and sliced
- ½ red pepper, deseeded and roughly chopped
- 1 small apple, ends and core removed (can leave skin on)
- 2cm piece of ginger, peeled and roughly chopped
- ½ red chilli pepper, deseeded and roughly chopped
- 2 large handfuls of unsalted cashews
- 2 tsp red Thai curry paste
- ½ tin (200ml) coconut milk (try to use equal quantities of the liquid and coconut cream layer at the top of the tin)
- 300ml vegan stock
- 2 tbsp lime juice
- Handful of fresh coriander, stalks included
- Salt and pepper, to taste

Optional toppings: chilli flakes, coconut flakes, coconut yoghurt, crispy fried onions, croutons, fresh chilli, sliced spring onion, vegan cream

INSTRUCTIONS

1. Place all the ingredients into a saucepan (apart from the lime juice, fresh coriander, salt and pepper).
2. Bring to the boil and continue to heat on a high simmer for 8 minutes, stirring frequently.
3. Remove from the heat and add the lime juice and fresh coriander.
4. Transfer to a high-speed blender and blend all of the ingredients together until smooth.
5. Add salt and pepper to taste.

SERVING SUGGESTIONS
—
Cheesy garlic bread, crusty bread, vegan cheese toastie, vegan noodles

CREAMY MUSHROOM SOUP WITH SHERRY & THYME

LEVEL: EASY | PREP TIME: 10 MINUTES | COOK TIME: 40 MINUTES | SERVES: 4

Don't underestimate the deliciousness of this creamy mushroom soup – it may sound basic but many of the Viva! team said this is one of their favourite soups! Dunk in a vegan cheese toastie and you're onto a winner!

SERVING SUGGESTIONS

—

Crusty bread, vegan cheese toastie, vegan cheesy garlic bread

INGREDIENTS

- **2 onions, finely diced**
- **1 tbsp fresh thyme leaves, stalks removed**
- **½ tsp ground or fresh nutmeg, grated**
- **500g mushrooms, sliced**
- **Pinch of salt**
- **2 cloves garlic, finely chopped**
- **2 tbsp plain flour**
- **1 litre vegan stock**
- **100ml vegan cream (any)**
- **3 tbsp vegan sherry or use vegan dry white or red wine (use alcohol-free versions or leave out entirely if preferred)**
- **Salt and pepper, to taste**

Optional toppings: caramelised onions, crispy onions, croutons, drizzle of truffle oil, fresh herbs (thyme, parsley, rosemary or chives), sautéed mushrooms, toasted or roasted pine nuts (see page 178), vegan cream or crème fraîche, vegan lardons, vegan Parmesan

INSTRUCTIONS

1. Fry the onion on a medium heat in a little oil until soft.
2. Stir through the thyme leaves, nutmeg, mushrooms and a pinch of salt.
3. Heat the mushrooms for around 5 minutes.
4. Add the garlic and fry for a further 2 minutes.
5. Stir through the plain flour, making sure everything is covered.
6. Pour in the stock, bring to the boil and then simmer for 20 minutes.
7. Transfer the soup to a blender and blend thoroughly until smooth.
8. Return it to the pan and add the vegan cream and sherry. Simmer for a few minutes and taste the soup, adding extra salt, pepper and nutmeg if needed.

GOLDEN BUTTERNUT SQUASH & MISO SOUP

LEVEL: EASY | PREP TIME: 10 MINUTES | COOK TIME: 30 MINUTES | SERVES: 4

One of the Vegan Recipe Club team went to a fancy restaurant in the US which used this unique combination of flavours, so we just had to share our own version. The umami from the miso and sweetness from the squash balanced each other beautifully and had the Viva! team hooked!

INGREDIENTS

- 1 butternut squash, peeled, deseeded and roughly cut into 2cm cubes
- 4 cloves garlic, finely chopped
- 1-2 white onions or 4 shallots, finely sliced
- 1 apple, peeled, cored and roughly cut into 4cm pieces
- 1 tsp chilli powder (optional)
- 850ml vegan stock
- 3 tbsp red miso paste
- Salt and pepper, to taste

Optional toppings: drizzle of chilli oil, fresh thyme leaves, sesame seeds, toasted or roasted pine nuts (see page 178), vegan cream or vegan crème fraîche

INSTRUCTIONS

1. Using a large saucepan, heat a little oil then add the squash, garlic, onion/shallots and apple. Cook on a low heat for around 15 minutes, stirring frequently.

2. Stir through the chilli powder and cook for a further 2 minutes.

3. Add the stock and miso, bring to the boil and then simmer until the squash is tender.

4. Remove from the heat and either blend using a stick blender or transfer to a high-speed blender and blend until smooth.

5. Try the soup and add salt and pepper to taste.

TOAST WITH ALL THE GOOD STUFF

LEVEL: EASY | PREP TIME: 5 MINUTES | COOK TIME: 5 MINUTES | SERVES: 1

This simple lunch involves taking a selection of your favourite ingredients and assembling them on toasted crusty bread with a dollop of delicious spread and a sprinkling of whatever you fancy – a great opportunity to get creative and be healthy at the same time!

INGREDIENTS

- **2 slices of crusty bread (ideally wholemeal or sourdough), toasted**
- **Choose from a layer of tahini, vegan cream cheese, vegan pâté, hummus or guacamole**

COOKED MIX
- **1 clove garlic, finely chopped**
- **Handful of cherry tomatoes, halved**
- **2 handfuls of fresh spinach**
- **Handful of marinated tofu pieces**
- **Pinch of salt and pepper**

COLD OPTIONS
- **1 avocado, sliced**
- **2 tbsp sauerkraut**
- **½ green or red chilli, finely sliced (seeds removed, optional)**
- **Handful of sprouted grains (eg alfalfa)**
- **Handful of mixed seeds (eg pumpkin, sesame, sunflower)**
- **Sprinkle of paprika or chilli flakes**
- **Drizzle of olive oil or essential vinaigrette (see page 167)**
- **Salt and pepper, to taste**

Alternative options: any salad ingredient, chickpeas, fresh herbs, fried kale, fried mushrooms, fresh basil pesto (see page 164) green goddess dressing (see page 164) kimchi, mixed bean salad, nuts, olives, peanut sauce (see page 168), toasted vegetables, rocket, sweetcorn, tahini sauce (see page 167) vegan cheese, vegan mayonnaise, watercress

INSTRUCTIONS

1. Heat a small amount of oil in a saucepan and then add the garlic. Fry for a minute before adding the cherry tomatoes, marinated tofu pieces and spinach.
2. Lightly fry for a few minutes and occasionally stir until the spinach has wilted.
3. In the meantime, slice all the vegetables and pop the bread in the toaster.
4. Put a layer of your chosen spread onto the hot toast and then layer up with the other ingredients, including the cooked ingredients.
5. Finish off with a drizzle of olive oil, dressing or sauce and a sprinkle of salt and pepper.

DIY POT NOODLE

LEVEL: EASY | PREP TIME: 15 MINUTES | SERVES: 1

The thing we love most about this lunch is that you can add pretty much anything you fancy to it! It's healthy, quick, easy and versatile which makes it perfect for work lunches or a dinner option when you're short of time.

INGREDIENTS

- 1 tsp miso paste
- 1 tbsp nut butter (optional)
- 1 tsp vegan stock powder or ½ vegan stock cube
- 1 tbsp toasted sesame oil (optional)
- 5 tbsp soy sauce
- Juice of ½ a lime
- 1 nest/large handful of instant noodles
- Handful of kale (big stalks removed), spinach or other greens
- 80g marinated tofu, deep-fried tofu puffs or firm silken tofu, cut into 1cm cubes
- 2 spring onions, sliced
- ½ carrot, grated or spiralised
- Handful of grated red cabbage
- Handful of frozen peas
- Green or red chilli, sliced
- Radish sprouts
- Toasted mixed seeds (see page 176)
- Handful of fresh coriander, stalks removed
- Sriracha sauce

Alternative options: any sprouts (eg alfalfa, mung bean, fenugreek), avocado, broad beans, broccoli stems, cauliflower, celery, chilli flakes, courgette, curry paste, edamame beans, fresh herbs, garlic, grated beetroot, grated ginger, green beans, mangetout, mushrooms, onion (finely diced), pineapple chunks (tinned or fresh), radish, sesame seeds, sliced red/yellow pepper, sugar snap peas, sweetcorn (tinned or fresh), tinned black beans, tinned chickpeas, yeast extract

INSTRUCTIONS

1. Prepare a one-litre mason jar with a lid, or thermos.
2. Put the liquids and pastes into the bottom of the jar and then fill the jar up in layers with your favourite combination of noodles, vegetables, seeds, sprouts, tofu etc or use the alternative options.
3. When you are ready to eat, fill the jar three-quarters full with boiling water straight from the kettle.
4. Stir thoroughly, put the lid back on and leave to sit for 10 minutes.
5. Stir again really well before eating, ensuring that everything has dissolved and is well blended.

CHEESY MUSHROOM OMELETTE

LEVEL: EASY | PREP TIME: 10 MINUTES | COOK TIME: 15 MINUTES | SERVES: 1

This vegan omelette is light, fluffy and so darn tasty that no one will know it was made without eggs! The black salt creates the eggy taste and the chickpea flour makes the perfect fluffy texture. The possibilities for fillings are endless, so mix things up and have some fun!

INGREDIENTS

BATTER
- 50g gram/chickpea flour, sieved
- 90ml water
- ¼ tsp black salt (Kala Namak) or use any salt
- ⅛ tsp baking powder
- Pinch of turmeric
- Pinch of black pepper

FILLING
- 100g mushrooms, sliced
- 50g vegan lardons or chorizo, sliced
- ½ clove garlic, finely chopped
- Pinch of chilli flakes (optional)
- 2 tomatoes, finely chopped
- Handful of spinach
- Salt and pepper, to taste
- 50g vegan cheese, grated

INSTRUCTIONS

BATTER
1. In a mixing bowl, thoroughly combine all the ingredients and set aside.

FILLING
1. Fry the mushrooms and vegan lardons/chorizo in a little oil until the mushrooms are slightly soft.
2. Add the garlic and chilli flakes and fry for a further 2 minutes.
3. Add the tomatoes and spinach and cook for a few minutes, until the spinach has wilted.
4. Remove from the heat and sieve out the liquid from the pan, leaving only the cooked ingredients.

OMELETTE
1. In a small-medium frying pan heat a little oil.
2. Pour in the batter, ensuring that it evenly covers the bottom of the pan.
3. Heat on one side until lightly golden.
4. Flip over and then add the filling to one half of the omelette. Sprinkle a little salt and pepper and the vegan cheese over the vegetables/vegan lardons.
5. When this side has cooked, fold the empty half of the omelette over the filling and serve.

SERVING SUGGESTIONS
—

Avocado, coleslaw, couscous, crusty bread, extra fried mushrooms, fresh herbs, fried asparagus, fried potatoes, hummus, olives, pea dip (see page 175), potato salad, quinoa, roasted red pepper dip (see page 172), roasted vegetables, rocket, salads, sriracha, steamed or roasted vegetables, vegan aioli, vegan mayonnaise

CRISPY POTATO & TOFU ROSTIS WITH CARAMELISED ONION CHUTNEY

LEVEL: NOT TOO TRICKY | PREP TIME: 10 MINUTES | COOK TIME: 5-10 MINUTES | SERVES: 4

Our former Food and Cookery Coordinator, Helen Wilson, developed this recipe and it remains one of the most popular dishes on the Vegan Recipe Club. Tucking into a crispy, golden potato rosti with the unique addition of tofu = win-win. We've added a caramelised onion chutney for extra pizzazz!

INGREDIENTS

ROSTIS

- 500g potatoes, peeled and grated
- 200g firm tofu, patted dry and crumbled into small pieces
- 2 handfuls of fresh spinach, finely chopped (or use frozen, defrosted)
- 2 cloves garlic, crushed
- 3 tbsp gram/chickpea flour, mixed with 3 tbsp warm water in a small bowl (mix and set aside)
- 2 tbsp plain flour
- Juice of ½ a lemon
- 1 tsp (heaped) caraway or cumin seeds
- 1 tsp chilli flakes (optional)
- 1-2 tsp salt
- ¼ tsp black pepper

EASY CARAMELISED ONION CHUTNEY (OPTIONAL)
Use a shop-bought version if short of time

- 4 red onions, sliced
- 70g golden caster sugar
- ¼ tsp salt
- 50ml red wine vinegar
- 50ml vegan red wine (use alcohol-free if needed)

INSTRUCTIONS

ROSTIS

1. Using a large bowl, add the grated potato and gently squeeze it against the side of the bowl before pouring away the excess liquid.

2. Add the crumbled tofu, spinach, garlic, gram flour mixture, plain flour, lemon juice, caraway/cumin seeds, chilli flakes, salt and pepper, then thoroughly combine the ingredients.

3. Shape the mixture into 8 round rostis – be firm but try not to over-handle. If they are too wet to hold their shape, add a little more plain flour.

4. Add a little oil to a large, non-stick frying pan and fry the rostis on a medium heat for 2-3 minutes on each side, until golden. Press down on the rostis and encourage them to keep their shape using a spatula.

EASY CARAMELISED ONION CHUTNEY

1. Using a large frying pan, add the onions, sugar and salt then heat on medium for around 10 minutes, stirring frequently.

2. Add the red wine vinegar and red wine then heat for around 20 minutes or until the liquid has reduced down and it has a sticky consistency.

3. Leave to cool then transfer to an airtight container or jar and keep refrigerated.

SERVING SUGGESTIONS
—
Coleslaw, crusty bread, cucumber, garlic bread, Greek salad, hummus or vegan mayonnaise, leafy green salad, mixed seeds, olives, potato salad, quinoa, tomatoes

BROCCOLI & TOMATO QUICHE

LEVEL: NOT TOO TRICKY | PREP TIME: 15 MINUTES | COOK TIME: 45 MINUTES | SERVES: 6-8

This quiche has been worked on and added to over the years, through the determined efforts of the Vegan Recipe Club team, and has turned into an absolute crowd-pleasing, mouth-watering success – please enjoy it as much as we do!

INGREDIENTS

PASTRY

For a quick version, use a 500g block of vegan ready-to-roll shortcrust pastry. Blind bake the pastry first if you prefer a crispier result.

- **250g plain flour (you can use half plain, half wholemeal flour for a healthier version)**
- **½ tsp salt**
- **115g butter, chilled and cut into pieces**
- **1 tbsp ground flaxseed mixed with 3 tbsp water in a small bowl and set aside for 5 minutes**

VEGETABLES

- **1 onion, finely diced**
- **2 cloves garlic, finely chopped**
- **1 small head of broccoli, broken into florets**
- **3 medium tomatoes, sliced**

FILLING

- **400g firm tofu, drained and patted dry**
- **225g savoury vegan cream cheese**
- **125ml unsweetened plant milk**
- **1 tsp mixed dried herbs or 1 tbsp fresh herbs of your choice (eg parsley, basil, oregano, chives), finely chopped**
- **1 tbsp Dijon mustard**
- **1 tbsp lemon juice**
- **3 tbsp nutritional yeast**
- **2 tsp vegan syrup (eg maple or agave)**
- **½ tsp turmeric**
- **1½ tsp salt**
- **Pinch of black pepper**

TOPPING

- **200g vegan cheese, grated**
- **250g cherry tomatoes, halved**

INSTRUCTIONS

PASTRY

1. Preheat oven to 190°C/375°F/Gas Mark 5.
2. Lightly grease a loose-bottomed, non-stick fluted flan tin.
3. Combine the flour and salt in a bowl then add the butter and flaxseed mix. Rub together with your fingertips until completely mixed and crumbly. Continue mixing until the dough comes together.
4. Transfer onto a work surface and continue kneading until a smooth dough forms. If the dough is too crumbly then add a tablespoon of water (only add bit by bit).
5. Roll out the pastry on a lightly floured surface to fit your tin. Spread the pastry evenly around the tin with your thumb and fingers. Trim the top and prick it a few times with a fork.
6. Place in the fridge to chill until needed.

VEGETABLES

1. Fry the onion in a little oil for around 5 minutes or until softened. Add the garlic and then fry for a further 2 minutes. Set aside.
2. Meanwhile, steam the broccoli florets for around 3-5 minutes until just slightly crunchy, not soft. Set aside.

FILLING

1. Using a high-speed blender or food processor, blend all the ingredients together until very smooth.

TOPPING/ASSEMBLY

1. Arrange the broccoli, tomato slices and onion/garlic mix around the pastry case evenly.
2. Pour the filling mixture on top, distributing it evenly with a spatula.
3. Evenly sprinkle the vegan cheese over the top then add the cherry tomatoes (seed side up) followed by a drizzle of olive oil.
4. Cover with foil and bake in the oven for 20 minutes.
5. Remove from the oven, take off the foil and place back in the oven uncovered for a further 20 minutes or until the top is slightly browned and the vegan cheese has melted.
6. Allow to cool a little before cutting and serving.

SUSHI DRAGON ROLL WITH SPICY TAHINI SAUCE

LEVEL: NOT TOO TRICKY | PREP TIME: 20 MINUTES | COOK TIME: 25 MINUTES | SERVES: 2

So, this is a combination of all of our favourite sushi dishes in one recipe! A dragon roll is basically inside-out sushi which is packed with a nori sheet wrapping, tasty fillings and a rice layer on the outside. We've covered ours with crispy onions and lashings of spicy tahini sauce – prepare to devour!

INGREDIENTS

RICE
- **130g sushi rice**
- **350ml water**
- **1 tbsp rice vinegar**
- **1 tbsp sugar**
- **½ tsp salt**

SPICY TAHINI SAUCE
- **½ clove garlic, roughly chopped**
- **3 tbsp lemon juice**
- **2 tbsp tahini**
- **1½ tbsp olive oil**
- **1½ tbsp water**
- **1 tbsp sriracha**
- **1 tsp syrup (eg maple or agave)**
- **Pinch of salt**

SUSHI/FILLING/TOPPING
- **1 large sheet toasted nori, cut in half lengthways**
- **½ carrot, peeled and cut into thin sticks**
- **¼ cucumber, cut into thin sticks**
- **½ avocado, finely sliced**
- **80g deep-fried tofu puffs or smoked tofu, finely sliced**
- **50g crispy fried onions**
- **20g fresh chives, finely chopped**
- **2 tbsp soy sauce**

INSTRUCTIONS

RICE

1. Using a medium-sized saucepan, wash the sushi rice 3 times, drain it thoroughly, add the 350ml water and then leave it to sit for 30 minutes (if you don't have time to leave it to sit, go ahead and cook straight away).
2. Place the saucepan of rice and water on the stove, bring to the boil, cover with a lid and then simmer for around 20 minutes or until the water has absorbed, checking occasionally.
3. In a mug, mix together the rice vinegar, sugar and salt and then pour it over the rice, mixing thoroughly. Set aside to cool to room temperature.

SPICY TAHINI SAUCE

1. Using a mug or jug mix all the ingredients together until smooth. Set aside.

SUSHI/FILLING/TOPPING

1. Ideally use a bamboo mat but if you don't have one you can use a sheet of greaseproof paper, cut a little bit bigger than the halved nori sheets.
2. Place a half sheet of nori, shiny side down, on the bamboo mat. Spread and cover the nori sheet with half the sushi rice. Press down firmly. Sprinkle with half the fried onions.
3. Flip the sheet over so the nori is on top and press down firmly again to help stick the fried onions to the rice. Place half the carrot, cucumber, avocado, tofu and a sprinkling of some of the chopped chives along the centre of the nori.
4. Roll the sushi into a cylindrical shape, packing it down tightly as you go. Cut into 6 even pieces.
5. Sprinkle the remaining chives (leaving half for the next roll) over the top. Drizzle over 1 tablespoon of the soy sauce followed by half of the spicy tahini sauce.
6. Repeat these steps to make the second dragon roll.

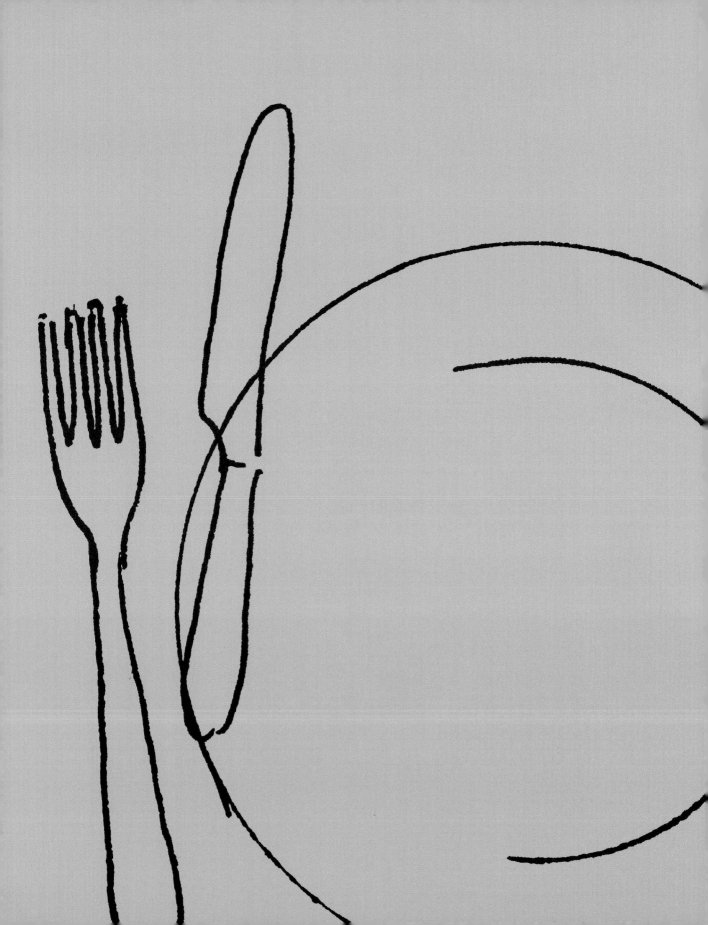

MAINS

One-pot pad Thai 77

Spicy coconut noodles 78

Vegetable paella 81

Classic moussaka 82

15-minute tofish with tartar sauce 85

Spicy protein burritos 86

Chilli non carne 89

Time is tight tacos 90

Create your own poke bowl 93

Jerk tofu with rice & peas 94

Pulled barbecue jackfruit with protein options & dirty slaw 97

Mac & cheese 98

Veg-packed spaghetti bolognese 101

Creamy one-pot carbonara 103

Spinach & vegan ricotta cannelloni 105

Vegan steak & ale pie 106

Mushroom bourguignon with white bean mash & kale crisps 108

Onion tarte tatin 112

Chestnut, mushroom & red wine pithivier 115

Prosecco fondue 116

SERVING SUGGESTIONS

—

Cucumber salad, lime wedges, pan-fried broccoli, vegan chicken satay, vegan Thai crackers, vegetable spring rolls (most are vegan but check the packet)

ONE-POT PAD THAI

LEVEL: EASY | PREP TIME: 2 MINUTES | COOK TIME: 10 MINUTES | SERVES: 2

This is one of the most popular recipes on Vegan Recipe Club! It's ridiculously easy to make, super-quick and tastes amazing – perfect for busy lives!

INGREDIENTS

- **300g (approx.) stir-fry vegetables of your choice**
- **150g (approx.) 'straight to wok' ribbon noodles**
- **2 handfuls of marinated tofu or marinated tempeh pieces**
- **1 handful of peanuts, roughly chopped**
- **1-2 tbsp peanut butter (smooth or chunky)**
- **3 tbsp soy sauce**
- **3 tbsp sweet chilli sauce (or use 2 tbsp syrup mixed with 1 tsp chilli powder)**
- **Juice of ½ a lime**

Optional extras: chilli flakes, fresh chilli, fresh coriander, toasted or roasted peanuts or cashews (see page 178), Thai basil

INSTRUCTIONS

1. Heat a little oil in a wok or large frying pan and add the stir-fry vegetables to the pan.

2. Fry for a few minutes before adding all of the other ingredients.

3. Stir frequently for a few minutes to ensure that the noodles are cooked and the peanut butter has softened and is evenly distributed.

4. Serve immediately.

TIP
—

For an alternative stir-fry sauce, remove the peanuts, peanut butter and soy sauce from the original recipe. Instead, heat the following ingredients in a small saucepan before pouring over the cooked stir-fry vegetables and noodles: 4 tbsp tahini, 2 tbsp syrup (eg maple or agave), 2 tbsp soy sauce, 1 tbsp rice vinegar, 1 tbsp lime juice, 1-2 tbsp sriracha, 3-5 tbsp water.

SPICY COCONUT NOODLES

LEVEL: EASY | PREP TIME: 10 MINUTES | COOK TIME: 15 MINUTES | SERVES: 2

We wanted to include a lovely fragrant, soupy dish and we couldn't decide whether to add a laksa, a ramen or this spicy coconut noodle dish. Due to it being one of the most popular recipes on Vegan Recipe Club, we just had to share this one with you – enjoy!

INGREDIENTS

SPICE PASTE

- Thumbnail of ginger, peeled
- 3 cloves garlic, roughly chopped
- 2 red chillies (seeds included), roughly chopped
- 2 stalks lemongrass, outer layer and ends removed and roughly chopped
- 1 tsp coriander seeds, ideally lightly toasted until they release their fragrance
- 1 tsp turmeric
- 1 tbsp neutral oil (eg rapeseed)

NOODLES

- 200g vegan noodles of your choice (we like soba)
- 1-2 onions or 4 shallots, finely diced
- 130g-150g mushrooms (mixed mushrooms work really well but any are fine)
- 500ml vegan stock
- 1 x 400ml tin coconut milk
- 200g spinach
- 100g deep-fried tofu puffs, halved or make ½ quantity of either tofu recipe on page 140
- Handful of fresh coriander, roughly chopped (optional)
- Juice of ½ a lime (optional)
- Handful of toasted or roasted cashews (optional – see page 178)

INSTRUCTIONS

SPICE PASTE

1. Blend all the spice paste ingredients in a high-speed blender or food processor until smooth(ish). You might need to add a little water or extra oil for blending. Set aside.

NOODLES

1. Cook the noodles according to the instructions on the packet, drain and set aside.
2. In a large saucepan or wok, fry the onion for 5 minutes.
3. Add the mushrooms and fry for a further 5 minutes.
4. Stir through the spice paste and heat for a few minutes, stirring frequently.
5. Add the stock and coconut milk, bring to the boil and then simmer for 10-15 minutes.
6. Add the spinach, tofu and the noodles and simmer for a further minute.
7. Remove from the heat (do not drain – it's supposed to be a slightly soupy dish), serve up and sprinkle with fresh coriander, lime juice and cashews (if using).

VEGETABLE PAELLA

LEVEL: NOT TOO TRICKY | PREP TIME: 10 MINUTES | COOK TIME: 40 MINUTES | SERVES: 4

This dish was originally labourers' food using rice and whatever vegetables were available in the nearby fields, cooked over an open fire. Since then, it's evolved into a much more elaborate dish but you can adapt it as you like depending on your budget, favourite vegetables and the occasion. The version below is a fancy one – delicious and perfect for dinner parties, garden gatherings or just plain old indulgence!

INGREDIENTS

- 1 onion, finely diced
- 120g vegan chorizo, sliced (optional)
- 1 red pepper, finely sliced
- 5 medium tomatoes, roughly chopped
- 2 cloves garlic, crushed
- ½ tsp smoked paprika
- ½ tsp cayenne pepper
- 200g paella rice
- 150ml vegan dry white wine
- Good pinch of saffron, soaked in tiny amount boiling water (ideally for 15-30 minutes)
- 450ml strong vegan stock (you might need to add up to 375ml more – see how you go)
- 2 bay leaves
- 200g frozen peas or broad beans
- 1 tbsp capers, drained
- 10 artichoke pieces (from a jar), halved
- 1 handful of olives, halved
- 1 tbsp fresh parsley or thyme leaves, chopped
- Salt and pepper, to taste

INSTRUCTIONS

1. In a paella pan, wok or wide frying pan, lightly fry the onion until slightly soft.
2. If using vegan chorizo, add this now and fry for a couple of minutes.
3. Add the red pepper and tomatoes and fry for a further 5 minutes, stirring frequently.
4. Stir through the garlic and fry for 2 more minutes.
5. Add the paprika and cayenne pepper and heat for 30 seconds before adding the paella rice.
6. Stir the rice through and fry for a minute before adding the liquid.
7. Add the white wine, bring to the boil and then reduce to a low simmer.
8. Stir through the saffron, stock and bay leaves and continue to simmer for 10 minutes. Don't stir whilst simmering.
9. After 10 minutes of simmering, add the frozen peas/broad beans but fold them in rather than stirring.
10. Simmer for another 10 minutes before adding the capers, artichokes, olives, seasoning and fresh herbs. Heat for 2 more minutes.
11. Serve immediately and enjoy with a glass of vegan wine.

SERVING SUGGESTIONS

—

Caesar salad (see page 41), fresh baguette, fried ripe plantain slices, garlic bread, garlicky green beans, leafy green salad, lightly fried asparagus, pan-fried broccoli (see page 148), roasted red peppers, vegan frittata or farinata

CLASSIC MOUSSAKA

LEVEL: NOT TOO TRICKY | PREP TIME: 15 MINUTES | COOK TIME: 2 HOURS 20 MINUTES | SERVES: 4

Recreate this heavenly dish and find yourself transported to the turquoise waters and tavernas of Greece. Enjoy layers of roasted aubergine and vegan mince in a rich tomato sauce topped with creamy béchamel and sizzling vegan cheese!

INGREDIENTS

AUBERGINES
- **6 aubergines, cut into 1cm slices**
- **Sprinkling of salt**
- **Olive oil**

FILLING
- **Olive oil**
- **2 onions, finely diced**
- **250g mushrooms, sliced**
- **3 garlic cloves, finely diced**
- **½ tsp dried or fresh oregano, stalks removed and finely chopped**
- **½ tsp ground cinnamon**
- **500g vegan mince**
- **2 tbsp tomato purée**
- **2 x 400g tins chopped tomatoes**
- **150ml vegan red wine**
- **150ml vegan stock**
- **1 tbsp vegan syrup (eg maple or agave)**
- **Salt and pepper, to taste**

BÉCHAMEL
- **4 tbsp vegan butter**
- **4 tbsp plain flour**
- **400ml unsweetened plant milk**
- **2 tsp Dijon mustard**
- **Pinch of ground or fresh nutmeg, grated**
- **1-2 tsp salt, to taste**
- **3 tbsp nutritional yeast**
- **2 tsp egg replacer powder (optional)**

TOPPING
- **200g vegan cheese, grated**
- **Sprinkling of vegan Parmesan (optional)**

INSTRUCTIONS

AUBERGINES
1. Preheat the oven to 200°C/400°F/Gas Mark 6.
2. Season the sliced aubergines with salt and drizzle with olive oil.
3. Place on baking tray(s) and cook for 20-30 minutes or until soft and golden, turning once.

FILLING
1. Fry the onion in a little oil until lightly golden.
2. Add the mushrooms and cook until slightly softened.
3. Add the garlic, oregano and cinnamon and fry for a further 1-2 minutes.
4. Stir in the vegan mince, tomato purée, chopped tomatoes, red wine, stock, and syrup. Bring to the boil, turn down the heat and simmer with the lid on for roughly 30 minutes, until most of the liquid has evaporated, stirring occasionally.
5. Taste the mixture and add salt, pepper and a little more syrup if needed.

BÉCHAMEL
1. Using a large saucepan, melt the vegan butter on a low heat.
2. Take the saucepan off the heat and stir in the flour until you have a smooth paste.
3. Return the pan to the heat, turn up to medium and very gradually add the plant milk, stirring continuously to avoid lumps.
4. Once the sauce has thickened, add the mustard, nutmeg, salt and nutritional yeast. Stir thoroughly and use a balloon whisk to get rid of lumps. Set aside.

ASSEMBLY
1. Reduce the oven heat to 180°C/350°F/Gas mark 4.
2. Place a layer of aubergine into a rectangular oven dish followed by a layer of the filling.
3. Repeat this process until you have several layers.
4. Leaving a little space at the top of the dish, pour over the béchamel sauce so that the top of the moussaka is completely covered.
5. Add the vegan cheese and top with a sprinkling of vegan Parmesan.
6. Cover the top of the dish with a sheet of foil and tuck in around the edges. Place in the oven for 25 minutes, then remove the foil and pop back in the oven for another 15 minutes or until the vegan cheese has fully melted.

SERVING SUGGESTIONS

—

Baba ganoush, courgette fries, crusty bread, flatbread, fried potatoes, fries, garlic bread, Greek salad, hummus, new potatoes, olive tapenade, potato salad, ratatouille, roasted courgette, steamed vegetables, stuffed vine leaves

15-MINUTE TOFISH WITH TARTAR SAUCE

LEVEL: EASY | PREP TIME: 10 MINUTES | COOK TIME: 5 MINUTES | SERVES: 4

Maryanne had a craving for tofish but didn't want all the fuss! She set herself the challenge of making it in 15 minutes and the results were amazing – enjoy this stress-free special!

INGREDIENTS

TOFU
- **500g firm tofu, drained and patted dry**
- **1 tbsp white miso paste mixed with juice of 1 large lemon in a small bowl**
- **Sprinkling of salt**
- **Small bowl of water**
- **10g (around 3 large sheets) toasted nori sheets**

BEER BATTER
- **Vegetable oil for deep frying**
- **400g plain flour**
- **3 tsp baking powder**
- **2 tsp salt**
- **550ml vegan beer, chilled (use alcohol-free or sparkling water if preferred)**

TARTAR SAUCE (OPTIONAL)
- **170g vegan mayonnaise**
- **1 shallot, finely diced**
- **1 tbsp capers, drained**
- **1 tbsp gherkins, finely chopped**
- **½ tbsp parsley, stalks removed and finely chopped**
- **½ tbsp dill, stalks removed and finely chopped**

INSTRUCTIONS

TOFU
1. Heat a large saucepan (just under) half full of vegetable oil on a medium heat or around 180°C and while you're waiting for it to heat up, start making everything else (keep an eye on it).
2. Cut the tofu into slices around 0.5cm thick.
3. Cover each slice of tofu with the miso/lemon mix then sprinkle them all with a little salt on both sides.
4. Tear off pieces of seaweed to wrap the tofu in (you don't need to be too careful or accurate about this).
5. Dip a single strip of seaweed in the bowl of water then wrap it around one of the slices of tofu. Repeat until all the slices have been wrapped.

BEER BATTER
1. Thoroughly combine the plain flour, baking powder and salt in a large bowl, then whisk in the beer until you get a smooth batter.
2. Dip a few tofu slices into the batter making sure they're fully covered. Lower carefully into the hot oil and fry until crisp and golden. Repeat this stage until all pieces are cooked.

TARTAR SAUCE
1. Stir all the ingredients together and decorate with a couple of sprigs of dill.

SERVING SUGGESTIONS
—

Baked potato, chips, coleslaw, courgette fries, couscous salad, curry sauce, dirty slaw (see page 160), lemon wedges, mushy peas, new potatoes, onion rings, peas, potato wedges, quinoa, rice, roast potatoes, roasted or steamed vegetables, salad, sweet potato fries, tomato sauce, vegan mayonnaise, vegan tartar sauce

SPICY PROTEIN BURRITOS

LEVEL: NOT TOO TRICKY | PREP TIME: 15 MINUTES | COOK TIME: 20 MINUTES | SERVES: 4-6

Well, who doesn't love a good burrito? We've worked hard to create a protein-packed, spicetastic taste sensation and they're easy to make too! Ideal for packed lunches or a speedy supper on busy weeknights.

INGREDIENTS

RICE
- **4 spring onions, ends removed and thinly sliced**
- **185g jasmine rice**
- **2 tbsp tomato purée**
- **500ml vegan stock**
- **2 tsp fajita seasoning**
- **½ tsp salt**

BEANS
- **1 green pepper, cored and finely sliced**
- **2 cloves garlic, finely chopped**
- **1 tbsp syrup (eg maple or agave)**
- **1 tbsp chipotle paste**
- **1 x 400g tin chopped tomatoes**
- **½ tsp salt**
- **¼ tsp black pepper**
- **1 x 400g tin black beans or kidney beans, drained and rinsed**
- **Juice of ½ a lime**
- **100g pecans, roughly chopped (ideally toasted or roasted – see page 178)**

SIMPLE TOMATO SALSA
- **2 medium/large tomatoes, diced**
- **1 tbsp lime juice**
- **Handful of fresh coriander, roughly chopped**

VEGAN SOUR CREAM
- **175g firm silken tofu (or any tofu, drained)**
- **1 tbsp lemon juice**
- **2 tsp neutral oil (eg rapeseed)**
- **½ tsp cider vinegar**
- **1 tsp syrup (eg maple or agave)**
- **¼ tsp salt**

TORTILLAS
- **4-6 wholewheat tortillas**
- **8-10 tbsp vegan cheese, grated**

INSTRUCTIONS

RICE
1. Using a medium-sized saucepan, heat a little oil before adding the spring onions. Heat for 3 minutes, stirring frequently.
2. Stir in the rice and tomato purée and thoroughly combine.
3. Add the stock, fajita seasoning and salt. Bring to the boil then cover and simmer on low for 15-20 minutes or until the rice is tender. Set aside and keep covered until needed.

BEANS
1. Using a large frying pan or wok, heat a little oil on a medium heat before adding the green pepper. Fry for 5 minutes, stirring frequently.
2. Stir through the garlic and heat for a further 2 minutes.
3. Add the syrup, chipotle paste, tomatoes, salt and pepper then simmer on medium for 10 minutes. Add the beans, lime juice and pecans and heat for a further 2 minutes. Taste the mixture and add more salt and pepper if needed.

SIMPLE TOMATO SALSA
1. Using a small bowl, combine all the ingredients and set aside.

VEGAN SOUR CREAM
1. Blend the tofu until it is completely smooth and has lost its grainy texture.
2. Add the remaining ingredients and blend until smooth.
3. Add a little more oil, salt, syrup or vinegar if needed.

TORTILLAS/ASSEMBLY
1. Splash a little bit of water onto the tortillas and microwave for 30 seconds or pop them under a medium grill for 30 seconds.
2. Lay the tortillas on a clean worktop then add 2 tablespoons of the rice mix per wrap, 2 tablespoons of the bean mix, 1 tablespoon of the salsa, 2 tablespoons of the sour cream and 2 tablespoons of vegan cheese. Of course you can add a little more or less of each depending on the size of your wrap or according to taste. Fold up the ends and roll up to seal.
3. Repeat until you have made 4-6 wraps in total. If you have any remaining filling, serve it with the tortillas.

TIP
—
If you're short of time, use shop-bought salsa instead of the homemade salsa and vegan crème fraîche or sour cream as an alternative to the homemade vegan sour cream.

CHILLI NON CARNE

LEVEL: EASY | PREP TIME: 10 MINUTES | COOK TIME: 40 MINUTES | SERVES: 4

We weren't sure whether to include a vegan chilli recipe or not as there are so many out there already, but it's such a classic and versatile staple we just couldn't leave it out. Serve with fluffy rice, cool vegan sour cream, guacamole and zingy lime for a taste sensation!

INGREDIENTS

- 1 onion, finely diced
- 2 sticks celery, sliced into 0.5cm slices
- 2 medium carrots, peeled and finely sliced
- 1 red pepper, deseeded and cut into bite-sized pieces
- 3 garlic cloves, finely chopped
- 1-2 tsp hot chilli powder or 1 red chilli, deseeded and finely chopped
- 1 tsp paprika or smoked paprika
- 2 tsp ground cumin
- 2 tsp ground coriander
- ½ tsp ground cinnamon or one cinnamon stick
- 1 tsp dried oregano
- 1 bay leaf
- 500g vegan mince
- 150ml vegan red wine (use alcohol-free if needed) or use extra stock
- 200ml vegan stock (use 1 vegan stock cube in 200ml boiling water)
- 1 x 400g tin chopped tomatoes
- 3 tbsp tomato purée
- 1 tbsp sugar or syrup (eg maple or agave)
- 1 tsp salt
- ¼ tsp black pepper
- 1 x 400g tin of kidney beans or black beans, drained and rinsed
- Juice of 1 lime

Optional toppings: fresh chilli, fresh coriander, guacamole (see page 25), jalapeños, salsa, sriracha, toasted seeds (see page 176), vegan grated cheese, vegan sour cream or vegan crème fraîche, vegan plain yoghurt

INSTRUCTIONS

1. Fry the onion in a little oil until soft (but not brown).
2. Add the celery, carrot and pepper and fry for a further 5-10 minutes.
3. Add the garlic and fry for 2 more minutes.
4. Stir through the spices and fry for another minute.
5. Add all of the remaining ingredients (apart from the kidney beans and lime juice), bring to the boil then leave to simmer for around 20-25 minutes, stirring occasionally.
6. Stir through the kidney beans and lime juice 10 minutes before the end of cooking time.
7. Taste the mixture and if needed, add more salt or syrup.

SERVING SUGGESTIONS

—

Avocado, baked potato, baked sweet potato, brown rice, burritos, chips, crusty bread, guacamole, potato wedges, quinoa, salads, steamed or roasted vegetables, toast, tacos, tortilla chips, vegan hot dogs, wraps

TIME IS TIGHT TACOS

LEVEL: EASY | PREP TIME: 15 MINUTES | COOK TIME: 1-10 MINUTES | SERVES: 4

Our former Food and Cookery whizz, Jane Easton, developed this wonderfully simple recipe and it's remained a firm favourite ever since! With a prep time of less than 30 minutes, this is definitely one to add to your list of weekly staples! A zingy combination of colourful fresh vegetables, protein-rich beans and tofu, and melty vegan cheese – what's not to love?

INGREDIENTS

- 1 x 400g tin black beans or kidney beans, drained and rinsed
- 225g (approx.) shop-bought or homemade salsa (see page 86)
- ½-1 tsp chilli powder
- 1 tsp ground cumin
- 1 tsp smoked paprika
- 1 red pepper, cored and diced
- 1 clove garlic, crushed
- ¼ red onion, finely diced
- 1 large tomato, diced
- Juice of ½ a lime
- 50g marinated tofu pieces
- 100g pineapple or mango (fresh or tinned), cubed (optional)
- Handful of jalapeños, finely diced (optional)
- Salt and pepper, to taste
- 8 taco shells
- 2 handfuls of vegan cheese, grated
- 1 avocado, cubed or mashed

Optional toppings: fresh chilli, fresh coriander, parsley, sliced spring onions, sweetcorn, vegan crème fraîche, vegan mayonnaise, vegan sour cream

INSTRUCTIONS

1. In a large bowl mix everything together (apart from the taco shells, the vegan cheese and the avocado). Add salt and pepper according to your taste.

2. Fill the taco shells with the filling and sprinkle the vegan cheese on top.

3. Either preheat the oven to 200°C/390°F/Gas Mark 6 and then place the filled tacos in the oven for 10 minutes or pop the filled tacos in the microwave for 1 minute (they won't be quite as crispy this way but it's quicker).

4. Add the avocado to the tacos and serve.

TIP

—

We like to drizzle teriyaki
sauce over the protein option
and then green goddess
dressing (see page 164) or
tahini sauce (see page 167)
over everything else –
it's a great combo!

CREATE YOUR OWN POKE BOWL

LEVEL: EASY | PREP TIME: 20 MINUTES | SERVES: 1

In this creative Hawaiian dish, 'poke' means 'cut into pieces' and involves gathering together whatever is on hand in the form of ingredients and dressings. We love the 'thrown together' quality of adding whatever you have in the cupboard and smothering it in a delicious sauce – healthy and lots of fun to make too!

INGREDIENTS

BASE
Choose 75g uncooked grains/noodles (then cook according to the packet) or use 150g pre-cooked grains

- **Brown rice**
- **Cauliflower rice**
- **Farro**
- **Millet**
- **Pearl barley**
- **Quinoa**
- **Soba noodles**
- **Sushi rice**

VEGETABLES
Choose a handful of some of these according to appetite, taste and budget

- **Avocado, sliced or cubed**
- **Carrot, grated or finely sliced**
- **Cherry tomatoes, halved**
- **Cucumber, diced**
- **Edamame beans**
- **Mango, cubed**
- **Pineapple chunks, drained and rinsed (if using tinned)**
- **Pre-cooked beetroot, cubed**
- **Radishes, sliced**
- **Red cabbage, grated**
- **Red onion, diced**

PROTEIN
Choose 1-2 of the following according to appetite, taste and budget
- **100g firm silken tofu, cut into 2cm cubes**
- **100g marinated tofu**
- **100g chickpeas or black beans, drained and rinsed**
- **100g deep fried tofu puffs, lightly fried until golden (only takes 2-3 minutes) then add 1 tbsp soy sauce**
- **100g vegan chicken pieces, cooked according to packet**
- **100g vegan tuna**
- **Make a half quantity of either tofu recipe on page 140**

TOPPING
Choose a sprinkling of 1-2 toppings (or as many as you like!)
- **Berries**
- **Chilli flakes**
- **Crispy onions**
- **Fresh herbs**
- **Jalapeños**
- **Mixed seeds (see page 176)**
- **Pickled ginger**
- **Pomegranate seeds**
- **Seaweed flakes**
- **Shelled hemp seeds**
- **Toasted or roasted nuts (see page 178)**
- **Vegan feta**
- **Wasabi peas**

SAUCE
Choose 1-2 sauces
- **Green goddess dressing (see page 164)**
- **Peanut sauce (see page 168)**
- **Sriracha mayo (1 tbsp vegan mayonnaise with 1 tsp sriracha)**
- **Tahini sauce (see page 167)**
- **Teriyaki sauce**
- **Vinaigrette (see page 167)**

INSTRUCTIONS

ASSEMBLY
1. Ideally use a wide bowl (but any will do) and then place your base option (eg rice, quinoa etc) on the bottom.
2. Arrange the vegetables into separate sections over the top, in a way that looks pretty (if you like!).
3. Place the protein option(s) into its own separate little section next to the vegetables.
4. Sprinkle over your topping(s) and then finally drizzle over your chosen sauce(s) – use as much sauce as you like.

JERK TOFU WITH RICE & PEAS

LEVEL: NOT TOO TRICKY | PREP TIME: 15 MINUTES | COOK TIME: 20 MINUTES | SERVES: 4

Bring the carnival to your kitchen with this hearty, protein-rich and delicious dish – comfort food at its best!

INGREDIENTS

JERK MARINADE

If you're short of time you can pour over a shop-bought jerk marinade, making sure the tofu is covered on both sides

- 2-3 cloves garlic, peeled
- ½ onion, peeled and roughly chopped
- Thumbnail of ginger, peeled
- 1 bunch spring onions, ends removed
- Juice of 1 lime
- 2 tbsp soy sauce
- 2 tbsp neutral oil (eg rapeseed)
- 2-3 tbsp brown sugar
- 2 tsp allspice
- ¼ tsp ground cinnamon (optional)

TOFU (MARINATING STAGE)

- 600g tofu (approx.), drained and patted dry then cut into slices around 0.5cm thick

RICE & PEAS

- 300g basmati rice
- 1 x 400g tin coconut milk
- 450ml cold water
- ¼ tsp allspice
- 2 sprigs thyme
- 1 x 400g tin kidney beans, drained and rinsed
- ½ tsp salt
- 1 bunch spring onions, ends removed and finely sliced

TOFU (FRYING STAGE)

- 6 tbsp soy sauce
- 6 tbsp nutritional yeast

INSTRUCTIONS

JERK MARINADE

1. Blitz all the ingredients in a high-speed blender or food processor until smooth. Don't be tempted to add water as the sauce needs to be thick.
2. Try the marinade and then add more sugar, soy sauce or lime juice if necessary, until the flavours are balanced.

TOFU (MARINATING STAGE)

1. Cover the sliced tofu in the marinade (on both sides) and rub it in. Leave in the fridge for a minimum of an hour, ideally (if you don't have time, you can use it immediately but the flavours won't have absorbed quite as much).

RICE & PEAS

1. Rinse and drain the rice using cold water.
2. Add all the ingredients to a medium-sized saucepan apart from the kidney beans.
3. Put the lid on the pan, bring to the boil and then simmer for 10 minutes.
4. Add the kidney beans after 10 minutes and then simmer for another 5 minutes with the lid off.

TOFU (FRYING STAGE)

1. While the rice is cooking, heat some oil in a large frying pan on medium heat and then add the marinated tofu slices to the pan.
2. Stir through the soy sauce and nutritional yeast.
3. Fry on both sides until golden.

SERVING SUGGESTIONS
—
Coleslaw, collard or spring greens, corn on the cob, fresh thyme leaves, fried plantain (fry slices of ripe plantain on either side in a little oil and salt), grilled pineapple, pan-fried broccoli, steamed or fried kale

TIP

Add some colourful mango salsa to your dish by mixing together: 1 large mango, diced; 1 large avocado, diced; ½ red onion, finely diced; 1 red chilli, deseeded and finely diced; juice of 1 lime; bunch of coriander, roughly chopped; drizzle of olive oil; salt and pepper, to taste; 1 clove garlic, crushed.

PULLED BARBECUE JACKFRUIT WITH PROTEIN OPTIONS & DIRTY SLAW

LEVEL: EASY | PREP TIME: 15 MINUTES | COOK TIME: 25 MINUTES | SERVES: 4

Even members of the team who said they didn't like jackfruit loved this dish! Jackfruit creates the perfect pulled meat substitute and we've added lots of spice, barbecue sauce and a selection of protein options for a hearty feast.

INGREDIENTS

SEASONING MIX
- **2 tsp sugar, ideally brown**
- **1 tsp paprika**
- **1 tsp chilli powder**
- **½ tsp salt**
- **½ tsp black pepper**

JACKFRUIT MIX
- **3 x 400g tins jackfruit, drained and rinsed**
- **1 red onion, finely diced (optional)**
- **2 cloves garlic, finely chopped (optional)**
- **180ml vegan barbecue sauce**
- **2 tbsp soy sauce**
- **100ml water**
- **Salt and pepper, to taste**

CHOOSE 1 OF THE FOLLOWING PROTEIN OPTIONS:
- **3 handfuls of salted cashews**
- **1 x 400g tin cannellini beans, drained and rinsed**
- **100g vegan lardons, cooked according to the packet**
- **Make a half quantity of either tofu recipe on page 140**

SLAW
- **Make a batch of our dirty slaw on page 160**

SERVING
- **4 large rolls spread with vegan butter**
- **Salad of your choice for serving**

INSTRUCTIONS

SEASONING MIX
1. Thoroughly combine everything in a small jug or mug and set aside.

JACKFRUIT MIX
1. Remove any hard pieces of core from the jackfruit and then shred/tease it apart well using your hands.
2. Place the jackfruit in a mixing bowl and coat with the seasoning mix. Set aside.
3. In a medium-sized saucepan, fry the onion in a little oil on a low heat until nicely caramelised (but not burnt).
4. Add the garlic and fry for another 2 minutes.
5. Add the seasoned jackfruit to the pan along with the barbecue sauce, soy sauce and water. Cook on a low-medium heat for around 15-20 minutes. Add salt and pepper to your taste.
6. Stir through the protein option of your choice and warm through for a couple of minutes.

ASSEMBLY/SERVING
1. Divide the jackfruit mix evenly between the 4 rolls.
2. Add the slaw and salad.

MAC & CHEESE

LEVEL: EASY | PREP TIME: 10 MINUTES | COOK TIME: 30 MINUTES | SERVES: 4

If you've never made a vegan cheese sauce using vegetables, then prepare to be amazed! The starchy potatoes, carrots and nutritional yeast combine to make a thick and deliciously tangy cheesy sauce. You can add anything you like to this dish to jazz it up, make it more healthy, colourful, protein-rich – get creative and enjoy!

INGREDIENTS

PASTA
- **300g macaroni plus water for cooking**

VEGAN CHEESE SAUCE
Use this sauce anytime you need a cheesy sauce, eg baked potato, nachos, pasta bake, vegan cauliflower cheese. You won't believe how delicious and cheesy it is!

- **225g carrots, peeled and sliced**
- **650-700g potatoes, peeled and roughly chopped**
- **125ml olive oil**
- **150ml water**
- **4 tbsp nutritional yeast**
- **2 tbsp lemon juice**
- **1 tsp miso paste (optional)**
- **2 tsp salt**
- **Pinch of black pepper**

Optional extras: black beans, breadcrumbs, fresh chilli, fresh herbs, fresh rocket, fried cherry tomatoes, fried mushrooms, garden peas (add to pasta 5 minutes before the end), guacamole, jalapeños, kidney beans, melted vegan cheese, mixed chopped nuts, mixed seeds, olives, onion, paprika, red pepper, steamed broccoli, sweetcorn, toasted or roasted hazelnuts or pine nuts (see page 178) vegan bacon bits, vegan chicken pieces, vegan Parmesan, vegan sausage, vegan tuna, wilted spinach (just add to the pasta a few minutes before end of cooking time)

INSTRUCTIONS

PASTA
1. Bring the macaroni to the boil and then simmer according to the instructions on the packet or to your preferred texture.

VEGAN CHEESE SAUCE
1. In a large saucepan, bring the potatoes and carrots to the boil and then simmer until soft (around 15 minutes).
2. Drain the water and then add them to a blender (using the largest blender jug).
3. Add all the other ingredients to the blender and then blitz until really smooth.
4. Pour the vegan cheese sauce straight over the pasta and stir through until fully covered.
5. Add any of the optional extras or enjoy the dish as it is!

SERVING SUGGESTIONS
—

Coleslaw, crusty bread, fresh salad, garlic bread, roasted cherry tomatoes, roasted vegetables, steamed vegetables (eg peas and broccoli)

VEG-PACKED SPAGHETTI BOLOGNESE

LEVEL: EASY | PREP TIME: 15 MINUTES | COOK TIME: 30 MINUTES | SERVES: 4

SERVING SUGGESTIONS

Bruschetta, focaccia, garlic bread, green salad, olives, pan-fried broccoli (see page 148), roasted or steamed vegetables, tahini sauce, tomato salad, vegan Caprese salad, vegan panzanella

We ummed and ahhed about whether to include spaghetti bolognese in the cookbook but it's one of the most popular recipes on the Vegan Recipe Club! We've taken a traditional approach with the added option of including tahini or nut butter to create a creamier sauce. You can use lentils instead of vegan mince and spiralised butternut squash, beetroot, courgette or sweet potato as an alternative to spaghetti. We're convinced this will become one of your weekly staples – enjoy!

INGREDIENTS

BOLOGNESE

- 1 large onion, finely diced
- 1 stick celery, finely sliced
- ½ red pepper, cored and diced
- 1 medium courgette, chopped in half lengthways then sliced
- 100g mushrooms, chopped
- 3 cloves garlic, finely chopped
- ½ tsp ground or fresh nutmeg, grated
- 225g vegan mince
- 2 x 400g tins plum tomatoes or chopped tomatoes or 400ml passata
- 125ml vegan red wine (use alcohol-free if preferred or 125ml boiling water)
- 2 tbsp tomato purée
- 1 tbsp syrup (eg maple or agave) or 2 tsp sugar (optional)
- 1 vegan stock cube dissolved in a tiny amount of boiling water
- 2 bay leaves
- 2 handfuls of fresh basil, stalks removed and finely chopped or use 3 tsp dried basil
- 2 tsp dried oregano
- ½ tsp salt
- ¼ tsp black pepper
- 1 tbsp tahini or nut butter (optional – to create a richer, creamier sauce)

SERVING

- 400g wholewheat spaghetti, cooked according to instructions on packet
- 8 tbsp vegan Parmesan or nutritional yeast
- Fresh basil for garnish

INSTRUCTIONS

BOLOGNESE

1. Fry the onion in a little oil until soft.
2. Add the celery, red pepper, courgette and mushrooms and cook until the mushrooms are golden brown.
3. Add the garlic and nutmeg and fry for a further 2 minutes, stirring frequently.
4. Stir through the vegan mince and heat for 2-3 minutes.
5. Add the tomatoes, red wine, tomato purée, syrup/sugar, stock, bay leaves, basil, oregano, salt, pepper and tahini/nut butter (if using).
6. Simmer for 10-15 minutes over a low-medium heat. Add a little water if needed.
7. Taste and add more salt and syrup if needed.

SERVING

1. Distribute the cooked spaghetti between 4 plates or pasta dishes then top with a serving of the bolognese. Finish with a sprinkling of vegan Parmesan or nutritional yeast and a garnish of fresh basil.

TIP

If you'd prefer to use lentils instead of vegan mince then use 2 x 400g tins green or brown lentils, drained and rinsed, then add them to the bolognese 10 minutes before the end of cooking time.

CREAMY ONE-POT CARBONARA

LEVEL: EASY | PREP TIME: 5 MINUTES | COOK TIME: 30 MINUTES | SERVES: 4

Comfort food at its best without the washing up – you're welcome!

INGREDIENTS

- 2 sprigs rosemary, stalks removed and finely chopped (optional)
- 200g vegan lardons or vegan bacon, diced
- 1 large onion, finely diced
- 200g mushrooms, sliced (optional)
- 3 cloves garlic, finely chopped
- 800ml vegan stock
- 150ml unsweetened plant milk
- 150ml vegan white wine (use alcohol-free if needed) or use 150ml extra vegan stock
- 250g dried spaghetti
- 200g frozen peas or fresh/frozen spinach (optional)
- Zest of 1 lemon, finely grated/chopped (optional)
- ½ tsp ground or fresh nutmeg, grated
- 250ml vegan cream or vegan crème fraîche (if you'd like extra protein then blend 150g silken tofu with the cream)
- Salt and pepper, to taste
- 50g vegan Parmesan or other vegan cheese or nutritional yeast

INSTRUCTIONS

1. In a large wok or saucepan, fry the rosemary with the vegan lardons in a little oil, according to the instructions on the packet. Remove from the pan and set aside.

2. Add the onion to the pan with a little extra oil and then fry until soft.

3. Add the mushrooms and fry for a further 5 minutes, stirring frequently.

4. Stir through the garlic and fry for 2 minutes.

5. Pour in the stock, plant milk and white wine then add the spaghetti. Bring to the boil and then simmer for around 15 minutes or until the pasta is soft and the liquid has absorbed. If using frozen peas or spinach add them around 5 minutes before the end of cooking time.

6. Stir through the lemon zest, nutmeg and vegan cream and heat for a further 3 minutes or until the excess liquid has absorbed.

7. Taste the mix and add salt and pepper if required then top with the vegan Parmesan or stir it through.

SERVING SUGGESTIONS

—

Bruschetta, Caesar salad (see page 41), courgette fries, crusty bread, garlic bread, green salad, grilled aubergine salad, olives, steamed or roasted vegetables

TIP

—

If you want to increase your protein intake, try adding silken tofu to a variety of dishes, eg béchamel sauce, curries, dips, other sauces, pasta sauces, salad dressings, smoothies and soups.

SERVING SUGGESTIONS
—

Ciabatta, fresh tomatoes, garlic bread, leafy green salad, lemon broccoli, olives, roasted aubergine, steamed or roasted vegetables

SPINACH & VEGAN RICOTTA CANNELLONI

LEVEL: NOT TOO TRICKY | PREP TIME: 25 MINUTES | COOK TIME: 65 MINUTES | SERVES: 6

Think cheesy, tomatoey, hearty, Italian deliciousness and you'll start to understand the appeal of this dish! Consistently one of the most popular recipes on the Vegan Recipe Club, it's well worth the extra effort and most people say it tastes exactly like the non-vegan version – our go-to crowd pleaser!

INGREDIENTS

CANNELLONI
- **14-16 cannelloni tubes**
- **Extra virgin olive oil**
- **400g spinach**
- **½ tsp ground or fresh nutmeg, grated**
- **1 onion, finely diced**
- **2 cloves garlic, finely chopped**
- **2 x 400g tins plum or chopped tomatoes**
- **Zest of ½ a lemon, finely grated/chopped**
- **Small handful of fresh basil**
- **½ tsp sugar or syrup (eg maple or agave)**
- **Salt and black pepper, to taste**

VEGAN RICOTTA
- **35g sunflower seeds**
- **450g firm tofu, drained and patted dry**
- **2 tbsp lemon juice**
- **1 tbsp olive oil**
- **¾ tsp salt**
- **Pinch of black pepper**
- **1 clove garlic, crushed**
- **20g nutritional yeast**

TOPPING
- **Handful of fresh basil leaves**
- **200g vegan cheese, grated**
- **Sprinkling of vegan Parmesan, grated (optional)**

INSTRUCTIONS

CANNELLONI
1. In a large saucepan, add the spinach, a drizzle of olive oil, half the nutmeg (¼ teaspoon), a pinch of salt and pepper. Cover the pan and leave the spinach to sweat and wilt down, stirring occasionally. Pop in a bowl and set aside.
2. In a large pan, fry the onion until soft and golden. Add the garlic and fry for a further minute.
3. Add the plum tomatoes and break them up with a spoon (or with your hands as you add them!).
4. Add the lemon zest, basil leaves and sugar/syrup. Simmer for around 20 minutes until the sauce has thickened. Add salt and pepper, try the sauce and add more until you get the desired seasoning.
5. While the spinach is sweating and the tomato sauce is simmering, make the vegan ricotta.

VEGAN RICOTTA
1. Blend the sunflower seeds in a food processor or using the milling blade on your blender.
2. Add the tofu and blend with the sunflower seeds until smooth.
3. In a bowl, combine the tofu/sunflower seed mix with all other ingredients and stir thoroughly.

ASSEMBLY/TOPPING
1. Preheat the oven to 180°C/350°F/Gas Mark 4.
2. Once the wilted spinach has cooled, thoroughly squeeze the liquid out of it and cut it up into small pieces. Add it to the vegan ricotta along with the rest of the nutmeg (¼ teaspoon) and stir until well-combined.
3. There are a couple of options for getting the vegan ricotta mix into the cannelloni tubes: either pipe it in using a piping bag or if you fancy having a bit more fun, then stuff the mixture in using your hands – kids love doing this!
4. Place the stuffed cannelloni tubes onto the bottom of an oven dish (30x25x5cm approx.). Pour the tomato sauce over the top and spread evenly. Add a layer of basil leaves then sprinkle over your vegan cheese, a sprinkling of vegan Parmesan and a drizzle of olive oil.
5. Cover the top of the dish with a sheet of foil and tuck in around the edges. Place in the oven for 30 minutes, then remove the foil and pop back in the oven for another 15 minutes or until the vegan cheese has nicely melted.

VEGAN STEAK & ALE PIE

LEVEL: NOT TOO TRICKY | PREP TIME: 15 MINUTES | COOK TIME: 60 MINUTES | SERVES: 4

This is a deliciously rich and hearty dish to have for a Sunday lunch or even to enjoy as a Christmas centrepiece. There are lots of vegan beef pieces available now but you can also use any vegan meat that you fancy – it will work just as well.

INGREDIENTS

- 640g vegan ready-to-use puff pastry sheets
- 1 onion, finely diced
- 1 stick celery, finely sliced
- 1 medium carrot, peeled and finely diced
- 200g baby button mushrooms, sliced in half
- 2 cloves garlic, finely chopped
- 1 tbsp tomato purée
- 2 bay leaves
- 1 tbsp dried or fresh thyme leaves, stalks removed
- 600g vegan beef pieces, cooked separately according to instructions on the packet
- 1½ vegan stock cubes, dissolved in a tiny amount of boiling water
- 550ml vegan sweet dark ale
- 2 tbsp vegan gravy granules, dissolved in a small amount of boiling water
- 2 tbsp soy sauce
- 1 tbsp sugar (ideally dark muscovado or other soft brown sugar)
- 2 handfuls of frozen peas
- Salt and pepper, to taste
- 2 tbsp unsweetened plant milk (for brushing)

SERVING SUGGESTIONS

—

Baked beans, boiled or mashed potatoes, cauliflower cheese (see page 152), chips, fresh herbs, gravy (see page 156), lemon Brussels sprouts (see page 151), mushy peas, mustard, pan-fried broccoli (see page 148), peas, roast potatoes, roasted or steamed vegetables, truffle fries (see page 143)

INSTRUCTIONS

1. Preheat the oven to 200°C/390°F/Gas Mark 6.
2. Grease either 4 foil pie cases (10cm diameter approx.) or 1 ovenproof dish (20-25cm diameter and 10cm deep) and line with puff pastry (if you don't have pastry cutters, use a knife or a bowl to cut out). Don't forget to keep some pastry spare for the lid! If you're using an oven dish, you don't need to line the bottom, just make a pastry lid using one of the pastry sheets.
3. Fry the onion in a little oil until soft.
4. Add the celery, carrot and mushrooms and fry for a further 5 minutes.
5. Add the garlic and fry for a further 2 minutes.
6. Add the tomato purée, bay leaves, thyme, cooked vegan beef chunks, stock, ale, gravy, soy sauce, sugar and frozen peas and simmer for around 10-20 minutes until the liquid has reduced down. If it reduces down too much, you'll need to add a bit more ale or water (you want the consistency to be thick but with a little excess liquid or it will dry out in the oven).
7. Taste the mixture and add a little more sugar if it's too bitter. Add salt and pepper to taste.
8. Remove the bay leaves and pour the mixture evenly into the pastry-lined foil cases or straight into the oven dish.
9. Place the lid(s) of the pie over the top and seal it to the bottom layer of pastry using your fingers. If using an oven dish then press the pastry lid into the sides of the dish.
10. Brush the top of the pie(s) with the plant milk before placing into the oven.
11. Cook for 20-30 minutes (approx.) or until risen and golden.

MUSHROOM BOURGUIGNON WITH CREAMY WHITE BEAN MASH & KALE CRISPS

LEVEL: EASY | PREP TIME: 20 MINUTES | COOK TIME: 40 MINUTES | SERVES: 4

Well, here's a deliciously simple take on a French classic. Enjoy a medley of mushrooms and herby goodness in a rich, gravy-like red wine sauce. Serve on a bed of our creamy white bean mash topped off with kale crisps and take your comfort food to the next level.

INGREDIENTS

BOURGUIGNON

- 30g dried porcini mushrooms, soaked in boiling water for 15 minutes (you can use 30g extra mixed mushrooms if you don't want to use any dried)
- 2 tbsp vegan butter (use oil if you prefer)
- 600g mixture of mushrooms, big ones halved and small ones left whole
- 125g shallots or pearl onions, halved or quartered if large
- 2 carrots, thickly sliced
- 120g vegan lardons or 2 handfuls of pre-cooked chestnuts, roughly chopped (optional)
- 2 cloves garlic, crushed
- 1 tbsp plain flour
- 1 tbsp tomato purée
- 375ml fruity vegan red wine (use alcohol-free if needed)
- 250ml vegan stock (use 1 vegan stock cube in 250ml boiling water)
- 6 sprigs of thyme
- 1 bay leaf
- Salt and pepper, to taste
- Handful of parsley, roughly chopped

INSTRUCTIONS

BOURGUIGNON

1. Heat 1 tablespoon of the vegan butter in a large saucepan on a medium heat. Add your mixture of mushrooms (but not the porcini mushrooms). Heat until cooked but firm, stirring frequently. Remove from the pan and set aside.
2. Add 1 tablespoon of vegan butter to the pan and add the shallots/onions, the carrot and the vegan lardons or chestnuts. Cook for 5-10 minutes, stirring frequently.
3. Stir through the garlic and cook for a further 2 minutes.
4. Pour in the flour and thoroughly combine with the other ingredients. Heat for 1 minute.
5. Drain the porcini mushrooms then add them to the pan along with the tomato purée, red wine, stock, thyme sprigs and bay leaf. Simmer on medium for around 20 minutes or until the liquid has reduced down significantly and you have your desired consistency. You can make your mash while the stew is simmering.
6. Add the cooked mixed mushrooms, stir and heat for 2 minutes. Add salt and pepper to your taste.
7. Top with fresh parsley.

INGREDIENTS

MASH

- **500g floury potatoes (eg King Edward or Maris Piper), peeled and cut into even chunks**
- **2 x 400g tins butter beans or cannellini beans, drained and rinsed**
- **2 cloves garlic, finely chopped**
- **2 tbsp vegan butter**
- **50ml unsweetened plant milk**
- **1 tbsp lemon juice**
- **1 tsp salt**
- **¼ tsp black pepper**

KALE CRISPS
Steam the kale if you prefer or serve with salad or other green vegetables

- **100g kale or cavolo nero leaves, hard/thick stems removed**
- **½ tbsp olive oil**
- **Very light sprinkling of salt**

INSTRUCTIONS

MASH

1. Place the potatoes in a large saucepan, cover with cold water and add a little salt.
2. Bring the potatoes to the boil then simmer on low-medium until tender but not overcooked. At 5 minutes before the end of cooking time, add the butter beans.
3. Drain the potatoes/beans in a colander and leave them to steam dry for a couple of minutes.
4. Fry the garlic on a medium heat, in a little oil for 2 minutes.
5. Add the potatoes/beans to a food processor along with the garlic, butter, plant milk, lemon juice, salt and pepper. Blend until really smooth (if you'd rather have more texture in your mash then use a potato masher instead of blending).

KALE CRISPS

1. Preheat the oven to 130°C/265°F/Gas Mark 1.
2. Lay the kale out onto a baking tray so the leaves don't touch.
3. Drizzle over the olive oil and salt then fully cover all the leaves (you might want to get your hands in there!).
4. Place in the oven for 15-20 minutes, or until crispy, turning once.

TIP
—
As an alternative, use the bourguignon as a delicious pie or pithivier filling.

ONION TARTE TATIN

This savoury version of a classic French dish is amazing! Caramelised, balsamic onions, white wine, thyme and vegan cheese make for an amazing combination of flavours. It works equally well at a summer dinner party, with new potatoes and green salad, or at a winter supper party with roast, sweet potatoes and seasonal green vegetables. Be prepared to demolish this in one sitting!

INGREDIENTS

- 300g vegan ready-to-roll puff pastry block
- 50g vegan butter
- Pinch of salt and pepper
- 1-2 tbsp thyme leaves, finely chopped
- 3-4 large onions, peeled and sliced into 2-3cm chunky rings (keep all of the rings whole)
- 60ml vegan stock (use 1 stock cube in 60ml boiling water)
- 1 tbsp balsamic vinegar
- 1 tbsp syrup (eg maple or agave)
- 60ml vegan white wine
- 100-150g vegan cheese (ideally vegan Parmesan), grated
- Unsweetened plant milk (for brushing)

Optional toppings: fresh herbs, toasted or roasted pine nuts (see page 178)

SERVING SUGGESTIONS
—
Cashew cheese sauce (see page 171), creamy mushroom sauce (see page 171), gravy (see page 156), green salad, grilled asparagus, new potatoes, roast potatoes, roasted vegetables, salads, steamed vegetables, sweet potato or celeriac mash, vegan cauliflower cheese, vegan crème fraîche

INSTRUCTIONS

1. Preheat the oven to 190°C/375°F/Gas Mark 5.
2. Roll the pastry out to around 0.5cm thick and cut a circle around an oven-proof frying pan (we used a 30cm diameter pan), leaving around 1cm excess around the edge. Put in the fridge while you make everything else.
3. Using your oven-proof frying pan, melt the vegan butter then add the salt, pepper and thyme. Arrange the onion rings in the pan. Cook them on a medium heat, on one side, for around 20 minutes until they start to get nice and brown.
4. Turn them over and add some chopped onion to fill in any gaps. Add some olive oil if needed and fry for a further 4-5 minutes or until this side has browned.
5. Pour the stock, balsamic vinegar, syrup and white wine over the onions. Cook until the liquid has reduced by half (around 5 minutes).
6. Remove the pan from the heat and then sprinkle the vegan grated cheese over the onions. Lay the puff pastry over the onions in the pan and tuck the edges of the pastry just underneath the onions by around 0.5cm (following the outline of the pan to keep a circle).
7. Brush the pastry with a little plant milk then place the pan in the oven and bake for around 20-25 minutes or until golden brown.
8. Remember the pan handle will be really hot (we've forgotten this a fair few times!) so use an oven glove or tea towel when flipping! Place a large plate over the top of the pan and flip it over allowing the tart to slide onto the plate, onion side up.

SERVING SUGGESTIONS

—

Cauliflower cheese (see page 152), creamy mushroom & white wine sauce (see page 171), fresh herbs, gravy (see page 156), mashed potato, roast potatoes, roasted vegetables, steamed vegetables, stuffing

CHESTNUT, MUSHROOM & RED WINE PITHIVIER

LEVEL: NOT TOO TRICKY | PREP TIME: 15 MINUTES | COOK TIME: 60 MINUTES | SERVES: 8

This traditional French dish, with its sunbeam pastry, is a feast for the eyes, rich, tasty, easy to create and makes for the perfect Christmas centrepiece or any time you're feeling fancy on a Sunday!

INGREDIENTS

FILLING
- 1 red onion, finely diced
- 2 leeks, ends removed and finely sliced
- 400g button mushrooms, halved
- 3 cloves garlic, finely chopped
- ½ tsp cayenne pepper
- 50g plain flour
- 2 tbsp tomato purée (or use harissa paste for a bit of spice)
- 200g vacuum-packed chestnuts, roughly chopped
- 2 tomatoes, roughly chopped
- 10 sundried tomatoes, finely chopped
- 1 tbsp dried or fresh thyme, stalks removed and finely chopped
- ½ tbsp dried or fresh rosemary or oregano, stalks removed and finely chopped
- 2 tbsp balsamic vinegar
- 175ml vegan red wine (use alcohol-free if preferred or mix 1 tbsp red miso paste with 175ml boiling water)
- 250ml vegan stock
- 1 tbsp soft brown sugar
- 250g pre-cooked quinoa or lentils
- Salt and pepper, to taste

PASTRY
- 640g vegan ready-to-use puff pastry sheets
- 2 tbsp unsweetened plant milk mixed with 1 tbsp syrup (eg maple or agave) for brushing

INSTRUCTIONS

FILLING
1. Fry the onion on a medium heat in a little vegan butter or oil until golden.
2. Add the leeks and fry for a further 5 minutes.
3. Add the mushrooms and fry for another 5 minutes.
4. Stir in the garlic and the cayenne pepper and fry for 2 minutes.
5. Stir through the flour until all the vegetables have been covered.
6. Stir through the tomato purée and add all of the other ingredients apart from the pre-cooked quinoa/lentils.
7. Allow the mixture to simmer, stirring regularly, for around 15-20 minutes or until the liquid has reduced down significantly (you don't want the mixture to be too runny).
8. Add the quinoa or lentils to the mix and stir through. The consistency should be thick but not too thick. Add a little more stock if necessary (you don't want it to be runny). Set aside until needed.

PASTRY
1. Preheat the oven to 190°C/375°F/Gas Mark 5 (ensure it's fully preheated).
2. Line a large baking tray with greaseproof paper and set aside.
3. On a floured surface, use a large dinner plate to cut one of the pastry sheets around the shape of the plate (this is your small pastry circle).
4. Place the smaller circle on the lined baking tray and set aside.
5. Take the next pastry sheet and again cut around the shape of the plate but this time leave 2cm of extra pastry around the edge (this is your large pastry circle).

ASSEMBLY
1. Transfer the mixture onto the small pastry circle and heap the mixture as high as possible, leaving at least 5cm of pastry free around the edge.
2. Cover the mixture with the large pastry circle and seal the edges with your fingers. Brush the edges with some oil.
3. To create the sun pattern, make a tiny hole in the top centre and then score wavy lines deeply (but not all the way through!) from the centre to the outer edge of the pastry using a sharp knife.
4. Brush the outside of the pastry with the plant milk/syrup mix until fully coated.
5. Place in the oven and bake for 25-30 minutes or until crisp and golden.

PROSECCO FONDUE

LEVEL: EASY | PREP TIME: 10 MINUTES | COOK TIME: 30 MINUTES | SERVES: 4-6

Get together with friends and family for this exquisite sharing dish! On a trip to Europe, one of our colleagues tried a celebrated vegan fondue – she highly recommended that we add some extra sparkle to this recipe by switching the white wine for prosecco – very happy to pass on the secret!

INGREDIENTS

- 350g potatoes, peeled and roughly chopped
- 125g unsalted cashews
- 1 onion, finely diced
- 3 cloves garlic, finely chopped
- 6 tbsp nutritional yeast
- 2 tsp Dijon mustard or white miso paste
- 1½ tsp salt
- ¼ tsp black pepper
- ½ tsp ground or fresh nutmeg, grated
- 1 tsp lemon juice
- 2 tbsp tapioca flour/starch (buy in health food shops, online and in global supermarkets)
- ½ tbsp syrup (eg maple or agave)
- 250ml vegan prosecco or vegan dry white wine
- 1½ tbsp kirsch or cognac (optional)
- 150g strong vegan cheese, grated (optional)

INSTRUCTIONS

1. In a large saucepan of boiling water, add the potatoes and cashews. Bring to the boil then simmer for 15 minutes. Drain and set aside.
2. While the potatoes and cashews are simmering, fry the onion in a little oil until golden.
3. Add the garlic and fry for a further 2 minutes.
4. Using a high-speed blender (using the largest blender jug), add the cooked potatoes, cashews, onion and garlic, along with all of the other ingredients (apart from the vegan cheese). Blend until smooth.
5. Using a large saucepan, pour in the mixture from the blender and add the vegan cheese. Bring to the boil then simmer for around 5 minutes or until the sauce thickens.
6. Either transfer the fondue to a fondue pot or serve straight from the pan.

SERVING SUGGESTIONS/ DUNKING

—

Avocado, boiled or roast potatoes, breadsticks, broccoli, cauliflower, cherry tomatoes, crusty bread pieces, gherkins, grapes, green apple pieces, mushrooms, smoked tofu cubes, tortilla chips, pasta (cooked), vegan mock meats (cooked)

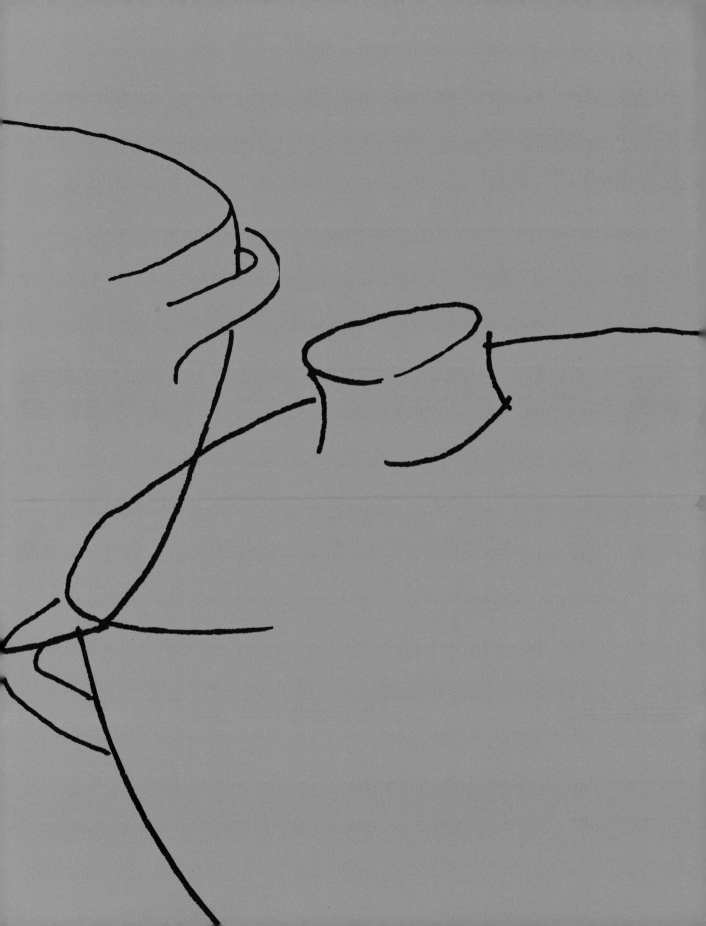

STEWS AND CURRIES

ONE-POT KALE, BEAN & LEMON STEW

LEVEL: EASY | PREP TIME: 10 MINUTES | COOK TIME: 10 MINUTES | SERVES: 4

This stew was created as a very quick, hearty, healthy meal which could be batch-cooked and frozen or popped in a flask for lunch the next day. What we didn't realise was that it was going to become one of the most popular recipes on the Vegan Recipe Club! The fennel seeds, lemon juice and chilli flakes really give this dish its unique flavour, so best not to leave them out.

INGREDIENTS

- **1 onion, finely diced**
- **2-3 cloves garlic, finely chopped**
- **1 tsp fennel seeds**
- **½ tsp chilli flakes**
- **3 medium carrots, sliced**
- **1 tsp sugar or syrup (eg maple or agave)**
- **1 x 400g tin chopped tomatoes**
- **600ml vegan stock**
- **1 tbsp red wine vinegar**
- **2 bay leaves**
- **180g kale leaves (stalks removed), sliced into 1cm strips**
- **3 x 400g tins butter beans, chickpeas or cannellini beans, drained and rinsed**
- **Zest of ½ a lemon, finely chopped**
- **1 tbsp lemon juice**
- **Salt and pepper, to taste**
- **2-3 tbsp nutritional yeast (optional)**

Optional toppings: drizzle of olive oil, fresh parsley, lemon wedges, nutrional yeast, vegan feta, vegan Parmesan, vegan plain yoghurt

INSTRUCTIONS

1. In a large saucepan or wok, fry the onion in a little oil until lightly golden.
2. Add the garlic, fennel seeds, chilli flakes, carrots, sugar/syrup and fry for a further couple of minutes.
3. Add the tomatoes, stock, vinegar and bay leaves and simmer on a medium heat for 5 minutes.
4. Pop in the kale, beans of your choice, zest and lemon juice and simmer for a further 5 minutes.
5. Taste the stew to make sure the carrots are soft then add salt, pepper and nutritional yeast, if required.

SERVING SUGGESTIONS

Crusty bread, garlic bread, green salad, mashed potato, potato cakes or rostis (see page 68), quinoa, rice, roasted or steamed vegetables, vegan feta, vegan plain yoghurt

GAMBIAN STEW WITH EASY PEANUT HUMMUS

LEVEL: EASY | PREP TIME: 5 MINUTES | COOK TIME: 55 MINUTES | SERVES: 4

Maryanne went to The Gambia and discovered a delicious peanut stew that was served everywhere. Determined to recreate this authentic dish for the Vegan Recipe Club, we now have one of our most popular dishes on the site! With a creamy, nutty sauce, colourful sweet potatoes and a lovely deep heat, it's easy to see why.

INGREDIENTS

STEW
- 1 large onion, finely diced
- 2 red or green chillies, deseeded and finely sliced
- 4 cloves garlic, finely chopped
- ½-1 tsp chilli powder (depending on how much heat you like)
- 2 tsp ground cumin
- 6 large tomatoes, roughly chopped or use 1 x 400g tin chopped tomatoes
- 200g smooth peanut butter
- 3 tbsp tomato purée
- 800g sweet potato, butternut squash or pumpkin, peeled and cut into 2cm cubes
- 800ml vegan stock
- ½ tsp salt
- ¼ tsp black pepper
- Juice of ½ a lemon

EASY PEANUT HUMMUS (OPTIONAL)
- 1 x 400g tin chickpeas, drained and rinsed
- 1 clove garlic, crushed
- 3 tbsp smooth peanut butter (use tahini if you'd rather make classic hummus)
- 2 tbsp olive oil
- ⅛ tsp ground cumin
- Juice of 1 lime or ½ a lemon
- ½ tsp salt
- ¼ tsp black pepper

INSTRUCTIONS

STEW
1. Fry the onion and the fresh chilli until the onion is soft and golden.
2. Add the garlic and fry for a further 2 minutes.
3. Stir through the chilli powder and cumin and cook for 1 minute.
4. Stir in the tomatoes, peanut butter, tomato purée and sweet potato before adding the stock, salt and pepper.
5. Bring to the boil and then simmer for 35-45 minutes until reduced and thickened and the sweet potato is soft (but not mushy).
6. Stir through the lemon juice and add more salt and pepper if needed.

EASY PEANUT HUMMUS
1. Using a high-speed blender or food processor, blend all the ingredients until smooth.

SERVING SUGGESTIONS
—
Brown rice, chapatis, crushed peanuts, crusty bread, fresh chilli peppers (remove the seeds for less heat or fry first), fried kale, garlic bread, hummus, leafy green salad, mixed seeds, quinoa, roasted or steamed vegetables, vegan plain yoghurt

CHEATIN' TAGINE WITH HERBY SALAD

LEVEL: EASY | PREP TIME: 10 MINUTES | COOK TIME: 30 MINUTES | SERVES: 4

Packed with golden aubergines, aromatic spices and sweet apricots, this tagine is inspired by the flavours of North African cuisine. We wanted to make it quick and easy for busy lives so created a cheatin' version just for you!

INGREDIENTS

TAGINE

- 3 aubergines, cut into 2cm cubes
- 2 cloves garlic, finely chopped
- 1 tsp ground cumin (optional)
- 1 tsp ground coriander (optional)
- ½ tsp ground cinnamon (optional)
- ½-1 tsp chilli powder (optional)
- 1 x 400g tin chickpeas, drained and rinsed
- 1 x 400g tin chopped tomatoes
- 3 tbsp vegan tagine paste
- 250ml vegan stock (add a little more if it's sticking to the pan)
- 2 handfuls of apricots, finely chopped or use 2 handfuls of raisins or sultanas
- 2 handfuls of green olives (optional)
- 2 preserved lemons, finely chopped (optional)
- Salt and pepper, to taste

HERBY SALAD (OPTIONAL)

- 2 tsp sugar (ideally brown)
- 2 tsp boiling water
- 3 tbsp olive oil
- 1 tbsp cider vinegar
- 2 white onions, finely sliced
- 1 large handful of parsley, stalks removed and roughly chopped
- 1 large handful of fresh mint, stalks removed and roughly chopped
- 1 large handful of fresh coriander, roughly chopped (remove stalks if preferred)
- Salt and pepper, to taste

Optional toppings: fresh coriander, fresh mint, fresh pomegranate seeds, tahini sauce (see page 167), toasted flaked almonds (see page 178)

INSTRUCTIONS

TAGINE

1. In a wok or large pan fry the aubergine on a medium heat, in a good amount of oil and a sprinkling of salt, until it is soft and lightly golden, stirring frequently.
2. Once the aubergine is lightly golden, add the garlic and fry for a further 2 minutes.
3. Add the spices (if using) and fry for a further 2 minutes.
4. Add all the other ingredients and stir thoroughly.
5. Heat on a medium heat for 15 minutes or until most of the stock has been absorbed and you have a nice, thick tagine.
6. Try the tagine and add salt and pepper to your taste.

HERBY SALAD

1. Using a mug or small jug, mix together the sugar and boiling water before adding the olive oil and cider vinegar. Set aside.
2. Take a salad bowl, add the onions, fresh herbs and seasoning then pour over the dressing.

SERVING SUGGESTIONS
—

Couscous, cucumber and red onion salad, loubia (Moroccan stewed white beans), pan-fried broccoli (see page 148), quinoa, roasted cauliflower (see page 147), roasted red pepper dip (see page 172), rocket salad with avocado and preserved lemon, saffron rice, tomatoes, vegan plain yoghurt or coconut yoghurt, warm flatbread or sliced pitta

BALINESE CHICKPEA & MANGO CURRY

LEVEL: NOT TOO TRICKY | PREP TIME: 10 MINUTES | COOK TIME: 30 MINUTES | SERVES: 6

This curry has flavours unique to Bali – enjoy a fragrant blend of kaffir lime, lemongrass, coconut and coriander with a choice of chickpeas or vegan chicken for protein and a mango twist!

INGREDIENTS

PASTE
- 1 red onion, diced
- 2 cloves garlic, roughly chopped
- 2cm piece of ginger, peeled and grated
- 1 red chilli, deseeded and finely chopped
- 2 tbsp neutral oil (eg rapeseed)
- 45g cashew nuts (ideally toasted or roasted – see page 178)
- 4 kaffir lime leaves
- 1 tsp ground coriander
- ½ tsp turmeric
- 1 tsp chilli powder
- Juice of ½ a lime

CURRY
- 1 x 400ml tin coconut milk
- 1 tsp salt
- 1 tbsp sugar (ideally soft brown) or 1 tbsp syrup (eg maple or agave)
- 2 x 400g tins chickpeas, drained and rinsed or use 280g (approx.) plain vegan chicken pieces or make 1 quantity of either tofu recipe on page 140
- 1 ripe mango, stone/skin removed and cut into small bite-sized cubes (or use around 150g pre-cut mango pieces, chopped into smaller cubes)
- 2 sticks lemongrass, bashed all the way along using rolling pin or similar (optional, but it adds incredible fragrance and flavour)
- Juice of ½ a lime
- Bunch of fresh coriander, finely chopped

Optional toppings: cashews (ideally toasted or roasted – see page 178), coconut yoghurt, fresh chilli, fresh coriander

INSTRUCTIONS

PASTE
1. Lightly fry the onion until soft. Add the garlic, ginger and chilli and fry for a further few minutes.
2. Transfer to a food processor or high-speed blender and add all of the other paste ingredients. Blend until nearly smooth. Add water or a little more oil if needed.

CURRY
1. In a large wok or deep frying pan, heat a little oil on a medium heat before adding the curry paste.
2. Cook and stir the paste for 1-3 minutes until the fragrance is released.
3. Stir in the coconut milk, salt and sugar and bring to the boil.
4. Add the chickpeas or vegan chicken pieces then turn down to a low heat.
5. Add the mango and lemongrass and simmer for 15-20 minutes.
6. Stir through the lime juice and fresh coriander at the end of cooking.
7. Taste the curry and then add a little more salt, sugar or lime juice if needed.

SERVING SUGGESTIONS
—
Cabbage salad with sesame dressing, coconut rice, pan-fried broccoli (see page 148), roasted or steamed vegetables, steamed or pan-fried pak choy, vegan Thai crackers, vegetable pakora, vegetable spring rolls, wilted spinach

SERVING SUGGESTIONS
—

Asian slaw, brown rice, jasmine rice, lime wedges, quinoa, steamed or pan-fried pak choy, vegan spring rolls, vegan Thai crackers

MASSAMAN CURRY

LEVEL: NOT TOO TRICKY | PREP TIME: 15 MINUTES | COOK TIME: 45 MINUTES | SERVES: 4

This recipe is a glorious mash up – a rich, flavoursome Thai curry with Indian and Malay influences. Tangy tamarind, fragrant lemongrass and aromatic spices combine with potatoes, tofu, red pepper and peanuts to create a unique and hearty dish.

TIP
—
For a quicker version, use 4 tablespoons of shop-bought vegan massaman paste.

INGREDIENTS

PASTE
- **1 tbsp coriander seeds**
- **4 cloves**
- **1 tbsp fennel seeds**
- **5cm piece of galangal, peeled**
- **2 sticks lemongrass, ends and outer layer removed then roughly chopped**
- **6 shallots, roughly chopped**
- **1 red chilli (including seeds), roughly chopped**
- **4 cloves garlic, roughly chopped**
- **3 tbsp neutral oil (eg rapeseed)**
- **3 tbsp water**
- **2 tbsp peanuts, ideally toasted or roasted (see page 178)**
- **Pinch of ground cardamom**
- **½ tsp ground or fresh nutmeg, grated**
- **Pinch of salt**

CURRY
- **Make 1 quantity of either tofu recipe on page 140 or use 250g deep-fried tofu puffs, cut in half – set aside**
- **1 onion, finely diced**
- **1 red pepper, deseeded and cut into small bite-sized pieces**
- **1 tsp chilli powder (only add if you like it really spicy)**
- **1 tbsp peanut butter**
- **1 white potato, peeled and cut into 2cm cubes**
- **1 sweet potato, peeled and cut into 2cm cubes**
- **3-4 kaffir lime leaves**
- **1 x 400ml tin coconut milk**
- **250ml water**
- **1 tbsp tamarind paste/concentrate**
- **3 tbsp soy sauce**
- **1½ tsp salt**
- **1 tbsp soft brown, palm or coconut sugar (or any sugar)**
- **Juice of ½ a lime**
- **Handful of fresh coriander or Thai basil, stalks removed and roughly chopped**

INSTRUCTIONS

PASTE
1. Place the coriander seeds, cloves and fennel seeds in a dry frying pan and heat them on a medium heat until they start to release their aroma, shaking the pan frequently. Remove and crush them using a pestle and mortar, spice grinder or blender. Set aside.
2. Add the galangal, lemongrass, shallots, chilli pepper and garlic to the pan with a little oil and heat for around 10 minutes, stirring frequently.
3. Place all of the paste ingredients (including the ground coriander seeds, cloves and fennel seeds) into a food processor or high-speed blender and blend until smooth(ish).
4. You might need to add a little bit more oil or water for blending.

CURRY
1. Fry the onion and red pepper in a little oil, on a medium heat, until the onion is soft.
2. Stir in the curry paste and chilli powder (if using) and heat for 5 minutes, stirring frequently.
3. Add the peanut butter, potatoes, kaffir lime leaves, coconut milk, water, tamarind paste, soy sauce, salt and sugar. Bring to the boil and then simmer on a medium heat for around 15 minutes or until the potatoes are soft but not mushy and the sauce has reduced down to your desired consistency.
4. Add the tofu and lime juice and heat for a further 3-5 minutes.
5. Stir through the fresh coriander or Thai basil and remove the kaffir lime leaves before serving.
6. Taste the curry and add more sugar, soy sauce or lime juice if needed.

TOFU KATSU CURRY

LEVEL: NOT TOO TRICKY | PREP TIME: 20 MINUTES | COOK TIME: 45 MINUTES | SERVES: 4

We absolutely love the Japanese flavours in this dish! The panko breadcrumbs create a satisfying golden crunch, complemented by a creamy katsu sauce. If you'd like a healthier version, then you can bake the tofu rather than deep frying.

INGREDIENTS

RICE
- 400g brown/ wholegrain rice, cooked according to the instructions on the packet

SAUCE
- 2 onions, finely diced
- 4 carrots, peeled and sliced
- 5 cloves garlic, finely chopped
- 4 tbsp plain flour
- 2 tbsp medium curry powder
- 1 tsp garam masala
- 1200ml vegan stock
- 2 tbsp soy sauce
- 1 tbsp syrup (eg maple or agave)
- 2 bay leaves

TOFU
- 2 x 400g blocks (approx.) firm tofu, drained and patted dry
- 5 tbsp plain flour
- 5 tbsp water
- 240g panko breadcrumbs
- Vegetable oil for deep frying

INSTRUCTIONS

SAUCE
1. While the rice is cooking, fry the onion in a little oil until soft and golden.
2. Add the carrots and sweat for 10-15 minutes (with the lid on) until they soften and begin to caramelise.
3. Add the garlic and stir for a further 2 minutes.
4. Stir in the flour, curry powder and garam masala and cook for 1 minute.
5. Pour in the stock slowly and gradually to avoid lumps.
6. Add the soy sauce, vegan syrup and bay leaves. Bring to the boil then reduce the heat and simmer for 20-30 minutes so the sauce has thickened but is still pouring consistency.
7. You can either keep the sauce chunky or pass it through a sieve if you'd prefer it smooth.

TOFU
1. Slice each block of tofu in half lengthways and set aside.
3. Mix the flour and water into a paste in a wide bowl and set aside. Add a little more flour or water if necessary, to create a thick, smooth paste.
4. Empty the panko breadcrumbs into a separate wide bowl and set aside.
5. Dip each chunk of tofu into the flour/water paste and make sure it is thoroughly coated.
6. Immediately dip the tofu chunks into the bowl of panko breadcrumbs. Again cover thoroughly, pressing the breadcrumbs into the tofu.
7. If you don't want to deep fry your tofu then heat the oven to 180°C/350°F/Gas Mark 4 and cook for 20 minutes, or until golden, turning once.
8. Otherwise heat a medium saucepan half full (no more) of vegetable oil on a medium-high heat or use a deep fat fryer.
9. Lower the tofu chunks into the hot fat and cook for a few minutes or until golden brown and crisp.
10. Remove each piece with a metal slotted turner and place on kitchen roll to soak up the excess oil until ready to serve.

ASSEMBLY
1. Divide the rice between 4 wide bowls or plates.
2. Slice the tofu then divide between the plates and place over the bed of rice. Drizzle with the curry sauce.

SERVING SUGGESTIONS

—

Crunchy slaw, cucumber with chilli oil, edamame beans, fresh chillies, fresh coriander, kimchi, leafy green salad, lime wedges, pan-fried broccoli with sesame oil, pickled radish, quinoa, roasted or steamed vegetables, sesame seeds, sliced spring onion

TIP

—

For a bit of variation, try swapping the tofu for slices (0.5cm thick) of aubergine, butternut squash, courgette or sweet potato.

SERVING SUGGESTIONS

—

Aubergine chutney, brown rice, chana masala (see page 134), chapatis, fried potatoes, lemon wedges, lime pickle, mango chutney, onion bhajis, poppadoms, steamed or pan-fried broccoli (see page 148), roasted cauliflower (see page 147) vegan naan bread, vegetable samosas

AUBERGINE DHAL WITH CORIANDER DIP

LEVEL: NOT TOO TRICKY | PREP TIME: 10 MINUTES | COOK TIME: 45 MINUTES | SERVES: 4

A jazzed up version of a classic vegan dhal. Protein-rich, budget-friendly and downright delicious!

INGREDIENTS

AUBERGINE
- 1 large aubergine, cut into 2cm chunks
- 3 tbsp shop-bought vegan curry paste (optional)
- Pinch of salt

DHAL
- 1 white onion, finely diced
- 6 fresh curry leaves (optional)
- 3 cloves garlic, finely chopped
- Thumbnail of ginger, peeled and finely chopped
- 2 tsp cumin seeds
- 2 tsp ground coriander
- 1 tsp turmeric
- 1 tsp chilli powder
- ½ tsp ground fenugreek (optional)
- ½ tsp asafoetida (optional)
- 1 tbsp tomato purée or tamarind paste/concentrate
- 300g red lentils
- 825ml boiling water
- 1 x 400ml tin coconut milk
- 1½ tsp salt
- ¼ tsp black pepper
- Juice of ½ a lemon

CORIANDER DIP
- 100g fresh coriander, including stalks
- Handful of mint leaves, stalks removed
- 100g unsalted peanuts or cashews, ideally toasted or roasted (see page 178)
- 2 small green chillies, deseeded
- ¼-½ tsp salt
- ¼ tsp turmeric
- 3 tbsp lemon juice
- 2 tsp brown sugar or syrup (eg maple or agave)
- 2 tbsp olive oil
- 6 tbsp vegan plain unsweetened yoghurt

INSTRUCTIONS

AUBERGINE
1. Preheat the oven to 180°C/350°F/Gas Mark 4.
2. In a large bowl, mix the aubergine with the curry paste, a good glug of oil and a sprinkling of salt. Ensure that the aubergine is thoroughly and evenly coated.
3. Place the aubergine chunks on a baking tray in a single layer and evenly spaced, then place in the oven for around 25 minutes or until soft and lightly golden, turning once.

DHAL
1. While the aubergine chunks are in the oven, make the dhal.
2. Fry the onion and curry leaves in a little oil or vegan butter until golden.
3. Add the garlic and ginger and cumin seeds and fry for a further 2 minutes.
4. Stir through the other spices and fry for another 2 minutes.
5. Add the tomato purée, lentils, boiling water, coconut milk, salt and pepper. Bring to the boil then simmer on a medium heat for 25 minutes.
6. Add the lemon juice and heat for a further 2 minutes.

CORIANDER DIP
1. Make the dip while the dhal is simmering.
2. Place all the ingredients in a high-speed blender and blend until very smooth.

ASSEMBLY
1. Divide the aubergine chunks into 4 portions and serve them on top of the dhal. Serve the coriander dip on the side or drizzled over the top.

AUTHENTIC CHANA MASALA WITH TAMARIND CHUTNEY

LEVEL: NOT TOO TRICKY | PREP TIME: 20 MINUTES | COOK TIME: 40 MINUTES | SERVES: 4

Former team member Thilak Kumaraswamy grew up in Tamil Nadu in India and has been learning to cook delicious traditional dishes ever since she was a child. Here is one of her family favourites. We've added our own speedy tamarind chutney recipe for a little extra treat!

INGREDIENTS

CURRY
- 1 tbsp vegan butter
- 3 onions, diced
- 4cm piece of ginger, peeled and roughly chopped
- 3 cloves garlic, roughly chopped
- 1 tsp cumin seeds
- 2 bay leaves
- 6 ripe tomatoes, roughly chopped then blended or use 2 x 400g tins chopped tomatoes
- 1 tbsp tomato purée
- 2 x 400g tins chickpeas, drained and rinsed
- 50g unsalted cashew nuts
- ¼ tsp turmeric
- 1-2 tsp chilli powder
- ½ tsp garam masala
- 2 tsp salt
- 200ml water
- 1 tbsp sugar
- 2 tbsp lemon juice
- Handful of fresh coriander, roughly chopped

SPEEDY TAMARIND CHUTNEY (OPTIONAL)
- 12 dates (ideally Medjool), pitted and soaked in boiling water for 10 minutes
- 2 tbsp tamarind concentrate/paste
- 1 tbsp dark or light muscovado sugar (or use any sugar)
- ½ tsp black salt (Kala Namak)
- ½ tsp regular salt
- ½ tsp ground cumin
- ½ tsp ground ginger
- ¼ tsp chilli powder
- ¼ tsp black pepper
- 8-10 tbsp water

INSTRUCTIONS

CURRY
1. Heat the vegan butter in a large frying pan or wok then add the onions. Fry them on a medium heat until soft (but not browned) for 5-6 minutes, stirring frequently.
2. Remove the onions from the pan then transfer them to a food processor.
3. Blend the lightly cooked onions with the ginger and garlic until you have a smooth paste. Set aside.
4. Add 3 tablespoons of oil to the pan and heat on a medium heat for a couple of minutes. Add the cumin seeds and bay leaves and fry for 15-30 seconds before immediately adding the onion/garlic/ginger paste.
5. Cook the paste for 5 minutes, stirring frequently.
6. Add the blended tomatoes and tomato purée, bring to the boil then simmer for 10-12 minutes, stirring occasionally.
7. Blend the cashews with a small handful of the chickpeas and a little water until smooth. Add them to the pan, then immediately add the turmeric, chilli powder, garam masala and salt. Cook for 5-7 minutes, stirring occasionally.
8. Add the remaining chickpeas, water, sugar and lemon juice then cook for 5-10 minutes.
9. Top with the fresh coriander and serve.

SPEEDY TAMARIND CHUTNEY
1. Drain and rinse the dates then add all the ingredients to a high-speed blender or food processor and blend until smooth.

SERVING SUGGESTIONS

Aubergine pickle, baked potato, brown rice, chapatis, coriander dip (see page 132), dhal (see page 132), lime pickle, mango chutney, naan bread, onion salad, poppadoms, quinoa, stuffed paratha, tamarind chutney, toasted or roasted cashews (see page 178), vegan pakora, vegan plain yoghurt, vegan raita

VEGAN CHICKEN TIKKA MASALA

LEVEL: NOT TOO TRICKY | PREP TIME: 15 MINUTES | COOK TIME: 30 MINUTES | SERVES: 4

There's a vegan Indian restaurant in Viva!'s hometown of Bristol which has a whole menu of mock meats. We didn't think it was possible to create something close to their vegan chicken tikka masala, but we've come pretty close with this one! It's really worth making your own paste but if you're short of time you can always use one from the shops.

INGREDIENTS

TIKKA MASALA PASTE

Use this homemade paste, or for a speedy version, use 4-6 tablespoons of a shop-bought vegan tikka masala paste

- 2 cloves garlic, roughly chopped
- 5cm piece of ginger, peeled and roughly chopped
- 1 red chilli, deseeded and roughly chopped
- 2 tsp ground coriander
- 2 tsp ground cumin
- 1 tsp turmeric
- 1 tsp garam masala
- ½ tsp ground fenugreek (optional)
- 1 tsp cayenne pepper
- 1 tbsp smoked paprika
- 1 tbsp tomato purée
- 1 tbsp desiccated coconut
- 2 tbsp neutral oil (eg rapeseed)

CURRY

- 500g vegan chicken pieces or use 2 x 400g tins chickpeas, drained and rinsed or make double quantity of either tofu recipe on page 140
- 2 onions, finely diced
- 1 red pepper, cut into bite-sized chunks
- 1 x 400g tin chopped or plum tomatoes
- 1 tbsp tomato purée
- 1 tbsp ground almonds (optional)
- 1 tsp salt
- 200ml water
- 1 tbsp syrup (eg maple or agave)
- Juice and zest of ½ a lime
- 150ml vegan plain yoghurt

Optional toppings: fresh coriander, toasted flaked almonds (see page 178), vegan plain yoghurt or cream

INSTRUCTIONS

TIKKA MASALA PASTE

1. Using a high-speed blender or food processor, blend all the ingredients together until smooth. You may need to add a little more oil or water to get a smooth consistency. Set aside.

CURRY

1. Cook the vegan chicken (unless using chickpeas or tofu), as per the instructions on the packet and set aside.

2. Whilst the vegan chicken is cooking, take a separate large pan and fry the onion in a little oil until lightly golden.

3. Add the tikka masala paste and red pepper. Heat for 5 minutes, stirring frequently.

4. Add the tinned tomatoes, tomato purée, ground almonds, salt and water. Cover with a lid and gently simmer for 15 minutes.

5. Stir through the syrup, lime zest and juice, vegan plain yoghurt and the pre-cooked vegan chicken pieces, chickpeas or tofu. Heat for around 5 minutes before serving.

6. Taste the curry and add a little more salt if needed.

SERVING SUGGESTIONS
—

Aubergine pickle, brown rice, dhal (see page 132), fresh tomatoes, fried potatoes, leafy green salad, lime pickle, mango chutney, onion bhajis, onion salad, pappadoms, roasted cauliflower (see page 147), steamed or pan-fried broccoli (see page 148), vegan naan, vegan raita, vegetable pakora, vegetable samosas

SIDES

EASIEST TOFU RECIPE EVER

**LEVEL: EASY | PREP TIME: 3 MINUTES
COOK TIME: 10 MINUTES | SERVES: 4**

Tofu is really versatile and absorbs marinades really well. The recipe below is probably the quickest, easiest way of cooking tofu that we've found, at the same time as being ridiculously tasty. You can add it to a range of dishes or just enjoy it on its own as a snack!

INGREDIENTS

- 250g-280g (approx.) firm tofu, drained, patted dry and cut into 2cm cubes or use tempeh cut into 2cm cubes
- ½ tbsp toasted sesame or rapeseed oil
- 3 tbsp soy sauce
- 1 tbsp syrup (eg maple or agave)
- 3 tbsp nutritional yeast

INSTRUCTIONS

1. In a non-stick pan gently heat the sesame oil then fry the tofu until golden, turning frequently.

2. Add the soy sauce and syrup then fry for a couple more minutes.

3. Add the nutritional yeast and fry for a further minute.

4. Taste, then add a little more soy sauce and/or syrup if necessary.

CRISPY GOLDEN TOFU (THAT GOES WITH EVERYTHING)

**LEVEL: EASY | PREP TIME: 5 MINUTES
COOK TIME: 5-10 MINUTES | SERVES: 4**

Well, the title says it all on this recipe – it's simple, quick and goes with (almost!) everything. You can change up the seasoning depending on the dish or keep it nice and plain – the possibilities are endless.

INGREDIENTS

- 250g-280g extra firm tofu, drained and patted dry then cut into either 2cm cubes, slices or triangles
- 1 tbsp olive oil
- 3 tbsp cornflour
- ½ tsp garlic powder or granules (optional)
- ½ tsp paprika (optional)
- ½ tsp salt
- ¼ tsp black pepper

INSTRUCTIONS

1. In a large bowl thoroughly coat the tofu with olive oil (you might want to get your hands in there!).

2. In a mug or jug, mix the cornflour, garlic powder/ granules, paprika, salt and pepper.

3. Pour this evenly over the tofu and make sure each piece is completely covered.

4. Using a large frying pan or wok, heat a little oil on a medium heat.

5. Add the tofu and fry for a few minutes on each side or until crispy and golden.

Note: if you'd rather oven bake the tofu then preheat the oven to 190°C/375°F/Gas Mark 5 and line a baking tray with greaseproof paper. Lay the tofu on the baking tray and place in the oven for 20-25 minutes or until golden and crispy, turning once.

TRUFFLE FRIES WITH VEGAN PARMESAN & LIME DIP

LEVEL: EASY | PREP TIME: 10 MINUTES | COOK TIME: 30 MINUTES | SERVES: 4

Take your fries to the next level with a drizzle of ethically sourced truffle oil, vegan Parmesan and a lime mayo dip!

INGREDIENTS

TRUFFLE FRIES
- 1kg potatoes (eg King Edward, Maris Piper, Russet), rinsed and skins left on
- 4 tbsp olive oil
- 1½ tsp salt
- ½ tsp black pepper
- 3 tbsp truffle oil
- 2 tbsp thyme leaves, stalks removed
- 6 tbsp vegan Parmesan, grated (or use pre-grated)

LIME & TRUFFLE DIP
- 6 tbsp vegan mayonnaise
- 2 tbsp lime juice
- 2 tbsp vegan Parmesan, grated (or use pre-grated)
- 2 tsp truffle oil
- 1 small clove garlic, crushed
- Pinch of salt and pepper

INSTRUCTIONS

TRUFFLE FRIES
1. Preheat the oven to 215°C/420°F/Gas Mark 7.
2. Leaving the skins on, slice the potatoes in half lengthways, then in half lengthways again. Keep cutting lengthways to make 2-3cm wedges/slices. Try to make them all roughly the same size – it's important that they stay uniform in width more than length.
3. On a large baking tray, add the potato slices and then cover them in the olive oil, salt and pepper, ensuring that they're fully coated (you might want to get your hands in there!). Make sure they're in a single layer and evenly spaced before placing them in the oven.
5. After 15 minutes take them out, very carefully turn them and then coat them in the truffle oil, thyme leaves and vegan Parmesan.
6. Place them back in the oven for another 15 minutes or until crisp and golden. Don't worry if they are still looking a bit white and undercooked at this point – just leave them in the oven (keeping an eye) until they have nicely crisped up!

LIME & TRUFFLE DIP
1. In a small bowl, mix together all the ingredients until fully combined.
2. Dunk the truffle fries into the lime dip and enjoy!

SNAZZY STEAMED VEG

LEVEL: EASY | PREP TIME: 5 MINUTES | COOK TIME: 5 MINUTES | SERVES: 4

We all know how important it is to reach our daily quota of fresh veggies; so, we've created this recipe to make it not just more appealing but downright delicious! Add them as a side to pretty much everything and bask in the glow!

INGREDIENTS

- 400g (approx.) vegetables of your choice (cauliflower, broccoli, carrots, courgettes, green beans, peas etc), chopped to a similar size
- 3 tbsp vegan butter/spread or olive oil
- 4 cloves garlic, crushed
- Pinch of salt and pepper
- Juice and zest of ½ a lime or lemon (optional)
- Handful of fresh herbs (coriander, mint, oregano, parsley, thyme) stalks removed and finely chopped (optional)
- Handful of flaked almonds, chopped mixed nuts, hazelnuts, walnuts, pine nuts or pecans, chopped and ideally toasted or roasted (optional – see page 178)
- Drizzle of chilli oil or 1 tsp chilli flakes (optional)

INSTRUCTIONS

1. Steam the vegetables for around 5 minutes, until they are tender but with a tiny bit of crunch (definitely not mushy!).
2. While the vegetables are steaming, in a small saucepan melt the vegan butter or olive oil on a low-medium heat then add the garlic.
3. Fry the garlic for 2 minutes but don't let it brown.
4. Toss the steamed vegetables in the garlic butter, salt and pepper. Stir through the lime/lemon juice, zest, fresh herbs and nuts (if using). Top with chilli oil or chilli flakes.

ROASTED CAULIFLOWER WITH LEMON & YOGHURT DRIZZLE

LEVEL: EASY | PREP TIME: 10 MINUTES | COOK TIME: 30 MINUTES | SERVES: 4

There's nothing more delicious than crispy roasted cauliflower. You can use this recipe to make the plain roasted cauliflower or jazz it up with our yoghurt sauce and all the toppings. It works brilliantly either as a side together with a variety of dishes, as a tapas plate or simply to eat alone as a tasty treat!

INGREDIENTS

CAULIFLOWER
- **1 large cauliflower, cut into florets**
- **1 tsp salt**
- **¼ tsp black pepper**
- **3 tbsp olive oil**
- **2 tsp cumin seeds (optional)**

YOGHURT SAUCE (OPTIONAL)
You can use our tahini sauce recipe on page 167 as an alternative
- **250g vegan plain yoghurt**
- **1 clove garlic, crushed**
- **Zest and juice of ½ a lemon**
- **¼ tsp salt**
- **¼ tsp black pepper**

Optional toppings: dukkah, fresh coriander, fresh dill, mint, pine nuts, ideally toasted or roasted (see page 178), pomegranate molasses, pomegranate seeds

INSTRUCTIONS

CAULIFLOWER
1. Preheat the oven to 200°C/390°F/Gas Mark 6.
2. Evenly place the cauliflower florets on a large baking tray then thoroughly cover in the salt, pepper, olive oil and cumin seeds (you might want to get your hands in there!).
3. Place in the oven for 30-35 minutes, or until golden and crispy, turning once or twice.

YOGHURT SAUCE
1. Mix all the ingredients together in a small bowl.

TOPPING/ASSEMBLY
1. To serve the cauliflower, drizzle over the yoghurt sauce and any (or all) of the toppings.

SERVING SUGGESTIONS
—

Burgers, curries, falafel, Middle Eastern dishes eg tagines, pittas, wraps or sandwiches, potato dishes, roast dinners (without the yoghurt sauce and toppings), salads, soups, tacos, tapas

PAN-FRIED BROCCOLI WITH ALMOND PURÉE

LEVEL: EASY | PREP TIME: 10 MINUTES PLUS 30 MINUTES SOAKING | COOK TIME: 10 MINUTES | SERVES: 4

We challenge you to find a more delicious way to cook broccoli! Crispy around the edges, lightly charred and beautifully tender, it feels like a meal in itself. Serve with our almond purée and suddenly you have gourmet (but very easy) cuisine!

INGREDIENTS

ALMOND PURÉE
- 1 slice slightly stale white bread, crusts removed
- 100ml unsweetened plant milk
- 50g blanched almonds, ideally toasted or roasted (see page 178)
- ¾ tsp white wine vinegar
- 1 tsp white miso paste
- 1 clove garlic, roughly chopped
- 2 tbsp lemon juice
- 1 tsp syrup (eg maple or agave)
- ¼ tsp salt
- ¼ tsp black pepper
- 2 tbsp olive oil

BROCCOLI
- 1 large broccoli head
- Sprinkling of salt

SERVING SUGGESTIONS
—
Curries, mac & cheese (see page 98), Middle Eastern dishes, pies, pithivier (see page 115), quiche (see page 71), roast dinners, salads, soups, stews, tagines, tarte tatin (see page 112)

INSTRUCTIONS

ALMOND PURÉE
1. Tear the slice of stale bread into small pieces and place in a small bowl. Pour the plant milk over the top and squish the pieces of bread down into the milk so that it's entirely covered. Set aside for 30 minutes.
2. Place all the other ingredients into a high-speed blender and when the bread has soaked, add it to the blender. Blend until really smooth. Add a little extra olive oil or plant milk if the mixture is thicker than you would like.
3. Taste the purée and add a little more salt, pepper, syrup, lemon juice and vinegar if needed.

BROCCOLI
1. Cut off the majority of the chunky stalk from the broccoli, leaving a little bit of stalk remaining.
2. Cut the broccoli in half through the centre of the stalk. Cut in half again through the centre and then in half again to give 8 wedges in total. If the wedges are still really big then you can halve them again.
3. In a large frying pan (which has a lid), heat some oil on a medium heat. Leaving the lid of the pan off at this stage, add the broccoli wedges, sprinkle over a little salt, then fry the wedges on both sides until crispy and dark in colour.
4. Take the pan off the heat, add the lid and then leave the broccoli to steam for 5 minutes.
5. Serve either on top of the almond purée or with the purée to the side.

LEMON BRUSSELS SPROUTS

LEVEL: EASY | PREP TIME: 5 MINUTES | COOK TIME: 40 MINUTES | SERVES: 4

Poor old Brussels sprouts have a hard time impressing people but we think we might just have cracked it. We challenge you to try this recipe and then tell us you don't like sprouts!

INGREDIENTS

- **500g Brussels sprouts, ends removed and halved**
- **3 onions, peeled and quartered**
- **Zest of ½ a lemon**
- **Handful of thyme sprigs**
- **½ tsp chilli flakes**
- **Salt and pepper, to taste**
- **2 tbsp vegan Parmesan (optional)**
- **Juice of ½ a lemon**

INSTRUCTIONS

1. Preheat the oven to 190°C/375°F/Gas Mark 5.
2. In a large roasting tin, thoroughly mix the Brussels sprouts, onions, lemon zest, thyme sprigs, chilli flakes and salt and pepper with a good glug of oil (you might want to get your hands in there!).
3. Roast for 20 minutes, turn the sprouts and then sprinkle over the vegan Parmesan. Place the sprouts back in the oven for a further 10-20 minutes or until they are crispy and golden.
4. Once cooked, evenly coat the sprouts in the lemon juice and serve.

CAULIFLOWER CHEESE

LEVEL: EASY | PREP TIME: 10 MINUTES | COOK TIME: 35 MINUTES | SERVES: 6

This dish doesn't need much of an introduction – cheesy, creamy, comforting, hearty deliciousness! We haven't scrimped on sauce in this recipe – it's a flavour-packed béchamel topped off with gooey melted vegan cheese and crispy golden breadcrumbs.

INGREDIENTS

CAULIFLOWER
- 1 large cauliflower, cut into florets

BÉCHAMEL SAUCE
- 6 tbsp vegan butter/spread
- 6 tbsp plain flour
- 600ml unsweetened plant milk
- 1 tbsp English or Dijon mustard
- ¾ tsp ground or fresh nutmeg, grated
- 6 tbsp nutritional yeast
- 1½ tsp salt
- ½ tsp black pepper
- 50g vegan cheese, grated (optional)
- 2 tsp white wine vinegar (optional)

TOPPING
- 200g vegan cheese, grated
- 6 tbsp breadcrumbs (optional – we like panko)

SERVING SUGGESTIONS
—
Baked potato, bangers and mash, Christmas dinner, crusty bread, garlic bread, green salad, pies, roast dinner, steamed or roasted vegetables

INSTRUCTIONS

CAULIFLOWER
1. Preheat the oven to 220°C/425°F/Gas Mark 7.
2. Bring a large saucepan of water to the boil, then add the cauliflower and continue to boil for 5 minutes if you like it with a bit of bite or 7 minutes if you like it a little softer. Take out a piece and check that it's cooked to your taste. You definitely don't want it to be mushy.
3. Drain the cauliflower then tip it into an ovenproof dish in a single layer. Set aside.

BÉCHAMEL SAUCE
1. Using a large saucepan, melt the butter on a low heat.
2. Take the saucepan off the heat and stir in the flour until you have a smooth paste.
3. Return the pan to the heat, turn up to medium and very gradually add the plant milk, stirring continuously to avoid lumps.
4. Once the sauce has thickened, add the mustard, nutmeg, nutritional yeast, salt, pepper, vegan cheese and white wine vinegar. Use a balloon whisk to get rid of lumps if necessary.
5. Stir thoroughly then pour evenly over the cauliflower.

ASSEMBLY/TOPPING
1. Evenly distribute the grated vegan cheese over the cauliflower then sprinkle over the breadcrumbs.
2. Place the dish into the oven and then bake for 20 minutes or until golden and the vegan cheese has melted.

YORKSHIRE PUDDINGS

LEVEL: EASY | PREP TIME: 25 MINUTES | COOK TIME: 20 MINUTES | SERVES: 6

Get your Yorkshire pud fix with this very simple recipe! It is guaranteed to brighten up any roast dinner or Christmas spread without the fuss!

INGREDIENTS

- **Vegetable oil**
- **190g self-raising flour**
- **¾ tsp baking powder**
- **¾ tsp salt**
- **270ml unsweetened soya or almond milk**

INSTRUCTIONS

1. Preheat the oven to 215°C/420°F/Gas Mark 7.
2. Fill a 12-hole muffin tin with 2 tablespoons of vegetable oil in each hole.
3. Place the tray in the oven for 20 minutes to make sure the oil is super-hot!
4. After about 15 minutes of the oil heating, make the batter but only mix the ingredients together just before use.
5. Sieve the flour, salt and baking powder into a large mixing bowl. Gradually pour in the plant milk, whisking constantly.
6. Remove the heated oil from the oven and quickly pour 2 tablespoons of batter into each muffin hole. For the best shape, try to pour the batter continuously (you might want to measure the first one into a measuring cup then roughly copy the amount poured to make it quicker).
7. Put the tray straight back in the oven and cook for 20 minutes.

CARAMELISED ONION & RED WINE GRAVY

LEVEL: EASY | PREP TIME: 5 MINUTES | COOK TIME: 20 MINUTES | SERVES: 4

Everyone needs a delicious vegan gravy recipe up their sleeve and trust us when we say that creating your own from scratch makes all the difference! Well worth the extra effort, you can thank us later.

INGREDIENTS

- 2 red onions, finely sliced
- 4 cloves garlic, finely chopped
- 1 tsp Dijon or English mustard
- 1 tsp yeast extract
- 2 tbsp plain white flour
- 100ml vegan red wine
- 450ml vegan stock
- 2 tbsp soy sauce
- 2 sprigs fresh thyme
- 1 sprig fresh rosemary
- ¼ tsp black pepper
- 2 tbsp cranberry sauce or redcurrant jelly

INSTRUCTIONS

1. In a medium-sized saucepan, fry the onion in a little oil on a low heat until nicely caramelised (but not burnt). You might need to add a little extra oil.
2. Add the garlic and fry for another 2 minutes.
3. Stir in the mustard and yeast extract and heat for 2 minutes.
4. Add the flour and thoroughly combine with the other ingredients.
5. Pour in the wine, stock and soy sauce and add the thyme and rosemary. Bring to the boil then simmer for 10 minutes or until the gravy has thickened to your taste, stirring frequently.
6. Stir through the black pepper and cranberry sauce and heat for another 2 minutes.
7. Remove the rosemary and thyme sprigs before serving.
8. Either blend all the ingredients together until smooth, strain out the vegetables or keep it chunky.

SIMPLE SAUERKRAUT

LEVEL: EASY | PREP TIME: 5 MINUTES | FERMENTATION TIME: 5 DAYS | SERVES: 4

This fermented food is great for your gut so it's good to get a daily dose if you can! It goes beautifully with sandwiches, salads, stir-fries, baked potatoes, bangers and mash, burgers, hot dogs, poke bowls, vegan cheese and crackers, soups, stews, burritos, curries... you get the idea!

INGREDIENTS
- 1 white cabbage, finely sliced
- 2 tbsp sea salt
- ½ tsp caraway seeds
- 1 tsp black peppercorns

INSTRUCTIONS
1. Place all the ingredients in a large bowl, mix thoroughly, then set aside for 30 minutes.
2. Using your freshly washed hands, squish the cabbage and massage it until it releases liquid. You will need to do this for a few minutes so that there's enough liquid to cover the cabbage when placed in the jar.
3. Place the cabbage mixture into a sterilised jar along with all of the liquid. Try to press the cabbage down, making sure that the liquid covers it. Try weighing it down by placing some greaseproof paper on top, followed by a weight of some sort – don't close the lid.
4. Leave the sauerkraut to ferment at room temperature for 5 days, or longer if you'd like extra sourness.

TIP
—
Try using a smaller jar filled with water inserted into the bigger jar, to weigh down the cabbage.

TIP
—
Try jazzing up your sauerkraut by adding any of the following: fresh chilli, fresh dill, garlic, ginger, grated beetroot, grated carrot, grated celeriac, grated fennel, juniper berries, turmeric root.

DIRTY SLAW

LEVEL: EASY | PREP TIME: 10 MINUTES | SERVES: 4

This is the kind of slaw that you get in fast-food restaurants – and it is delicious! It goes great with pulled jackfruit, tofish and chips, barbecues and burgers! If you prefer it clean, replace the dressing with a little olive oil or sesame oil, lemon or lime juice and add toasted pumpkin, sunflower and/or sesame seeds (see page 176).

INGREDIENTS

VEGETABLES
- **180g white cabbage, grated (use half white and half red if you prefer)**
- **1 carrot, peeled and grated**
- **¼ white onion, very finely minced**

DRESSING
- **1 tbsp caster sugar**
- **3 tbsp vegan mayonnaise**
- **1 tbsp unsweetened plant milk mixed with 1 tbsp white wine vinegar or cider vinegar**
- **1 tbsp lemon juice**
- **½ tsp salt**
- **½ tsp black pepper**

INSTRUCTIONS

VEGETABLES
1. Place the grated vegetables in a mixing bowl and set aside.

DRESSING
1. Mix all the ingredients together thoroughly then stir through the vegetables until evenly coated.

TIP
—
If you want to posh up the coleslaw then thinly slice the cabbage instead of grating it and add one fennel bulb, cut into quarters and shredded.

TIP
—
If you'd like to create a Thai-style slaw then take off the original dressing and create a new dressing using the following ingredients: 2 tbsp olive oil, 2 tbsp toasted sesame oil, 2 tbsp syrup (eg maple or agave), 3 tbsp rice vinegar or cider vinegar, 1 tbsp soy sauce, 2cm piece of ginger, peeled and grated, 1 clove garlic, crushed, ½ tsp salt, ½ tsp chilli flakes.

SAUCES, DRESSINGS, DIPS AND OTHER ESSENTIALS

GREEN GODDESS DRESSING

LEVEL: EASY | PREP TIME: 10 MINUTES | SERVES: 2

It will come as no surprise that variations of this luscious 'get the glow' dressing originated in sunny California! Bursting with flavour and nutrients, there's lots to love about this versatile sauce!

INGREDIENTS

- 1 avocado
- 80ml water
- Juice of 1 lemon or lime
- 2 tbsp olive oil
- 15g parsley, stalks removed
- 2 spring onions, ends and outer layer removed, then roughly chopped
- 1 clove garlic, roughly chopped
- 1 tsp syrup (eg maple or agave)
- ½ tsp salt
- Pinch of black pepper

INSTRUCTIONS

1. Place all the ingredients in a high-speed blender or food processor and blend until smooth.

2. Store in an airtight container in the fridge for up to 7 days.

FRESH BASIL PESTO

LEVEL: EASY | PREP TIME: 5 MINUTES
SERVES: 3-4 (USED ON A PASTA DISH)

Why does pesto just make everything taste amazing?! Whilst the original combination is undeniably awesome, you can change things up by swapping the pine nuts for walnuts, pistachios or almonds (ideally toasted or roasted – see page 178) and try switching the basil for wild garlic, kale or even broccoli!

INGREDIENTS

- 50g pine nuts, ideally toasted or roasted (see page 178) or ground almonds
- 60g basil, stalks removed
- 1 clove garlic, crushed
- 5 tbsp vegan Parmesan or nutritional yeast
- 100ml olive oil
- 2 tbsp lemon juice
- ¼ tsp salt
- ¼ tsp black pepper

INSTRUCTIONS

1. Place all the ingredients in a food processor and use the 'pulse' mode to gently blend until you get your desired consistency. We like to keep ours chunky!

2. Keep the pesto in a jar or airtight container in the fridge for up to 5 days.

GREEN GODDESS SERVING SUGGESTIONS

—

Baked potato (or any potato of your choice), Buddha bowls, burgers, burrito bowls, grain bowls, hummus, pasta (including courgette spaghetti), poke bowls, potato chips, potato salad, quinoa or couscous, raw vegetable sticks, salad sticks, salads (including warm salads), sandwiches, tofu dishes, tortilla chips, vegan cheese toasties, vegan tuna or chickpeas

SERVING SUGGESTIONS

—

Couscous, garlic bread, gnocchi,
hummus, mashed potato, omelette,
pasta, pizza, risotto, roasted
vegetables, salads, sandwiches,
soups (especially pistou), stews,
toast, vegan cheese toasties,
vegan ravioli

THE ULTIMATE TAHINI SAUCE

LEVEL: EASY | PREP TIME: 5 MINUTES | SERVES: 4

We eat this all the time and add it to absolutely everything – yes we adore tahini! You can keep this sauce in the fridge for up to 7 days to spruce up all of your dishes.

INGREDIENTS

- 1 clove garlic, roughly chopped
- 100ml lemon juice (fresh or bottled)
- 4½ tbsp tahini
- 3 tbsp olive oil
- 3 tbsp water
- Pinch of salt

INSTRUCTIONS

1. Blend all the ingredients together until smooth. If the mixture is too thick, add a little more water and olive oil (do this a bit at a time as you don't want it to be runny).

SERVING SUGGESTIONS

Buddha bowls, burgers, chopped vegetables for dipping, falafel dishes, Middle Eastern dishes, pan-fried broccoli (see page 148), pasta, pittas, roasted cauliflower (see page 147), salads, sandwiches, soups, stir-fries, tagines, wraps

ESSENTIAL VINAIGRETTE

LEVEL: EASY | PREP TIME: 5 MINUTES | SERVES: 6

An essential recipe to add to your repertoire – make it in minutes and drizzle it on, well… everything!

INGREDIENTS

- 125ml olive oil
- 3 tbsp cider vinegar
- 1 tbsp Dijon mustard or 2 tsp English mustard
- 1 tbsp syrup (eg maple or agave)
- 1 clove garlic, crushed
- ¼ tsp salt
- Pinch of black pepper
- 1 tsp dried mixed herbs (optional)

INSTRUCTIONS

1. In a jug, mug or jar, thoroughly mix all of the ingredients together.

2. Keep in an airtight container in the fridge for up to 7-10 days.

SERVING SUGGESTIONS

Avocado/anything on toast (see page 63), pasta, potatoes (all kinds), salads and side salads, sandwiches, steamed or roasted vegetables, toasties, wraps

THE TASTIEST PEANUT SAUCE

LEVEL: EASY | PREP TIME: 5 MINUTES | COOK TIME: 5 MINUTES | SERVES: 4

Who doesn't like tangy peanut sauce?! Try pouring over Buddha or poke bowls (see page 93), drizzling over stir-fries or for dunking in tofu skewers – a firm favourite in the Viva! office!

INGREDIENTS

- 6 tbsp smooth peanut butter
- 2 tbsp rice vinegar (or use white wine vinegar or cider vinegar as an alternative)
- ¼ tsp chilli powder or 1 tsp sriracha
- 2 tbsp syrup (eg maple or agave)
- 1½ tbsp soy sauce
- Juice of ½ a lime
- 60ml water
- ½ garlic clove, crushed

INSTRUCTIONS

1. Either thoroughly combine all the ingredients in a bowl using a fork or balloon whisk or blend using a high-speed blender.
2. You can serve the sauce hot or cold.

IF HEATING

1. Place the sauce in a saucepan, add a little more water (around 50ml) then gently heat for around 5 minutes or until warmed through, stirring frequently.

SERVING SUGGESTIONS
—

Buddha bowls, burgers, grain bowls, noodle dishes, poke bowls, raw vegetable sticks, rice dishes, spring rolls, stir-fries, summer rolls, tofu or vegan chicken satay sticks

SERVING SUGGESTIONS

—

Baked potato, Buddha bowls, burritos, cauliflower cheese, chips, hot dogs, mashed potato, nachos, nut roast, pasta, pizza, poke bowls, risotto, roast dinner, roasted or steamed vegetables, soups, stews, tacos, tarte tatin (see page 112), vegan meatballs

CASHEW CHEESE SAUCE

LEVEL: EASY | PREP TIME: 15 MINUTES SERVES: 4-6

This is such a nutritious, protein-rich and tasty cheese sauce which can be used for a huge variety of dishes. A must-have classic to add to your repertoire!

INGREDIENTS

- 200g cashews, soaked in boiling water for minimum 10 minutes
- 1 clove garlic, crushed
- 2 tbsp lemon juice
- 2 tbsp nutritional yeast (add 1 extra tbsp if you like it super cheesy)
- 1 tsp salt
- ¼ tsp black pepper
- 1 tsp white miso paste
- 1 tsp Dijon mustard
- 2 tsp sriracha (optional)
- 200ml water (use boiling water to serve it hot)

INSTRUCTIONS

1. Drain and rinse the cashews.
2. Using a high-speed blender, blend all the ingredients together until very smooth.
3. If you need to reheat the sauce, warm it in a saucepan on a medium heat for 5 minutes. You might need to add a little more water if reheating.

MUSHROOM SAUCE SERVING SUGGESTIONS

—

As a pie filling, baked potato, nut roast, pasta, pies, pithivier, (see page 115) rice, roast dinner, tarte tatin (see page 112), vegan chicken, vegan fish fillet, vegan sausage and mash, vegan steak

CREAMY WHITE WINE MUSHROOM SAUCE

LEVEL: EASY | PREP TIME: 5 MINUTES
COOK TIME: 20 MINUTES | SERVES: 4

It's very handy to have this deliciously creamy sauce recipe up your sleeve as it goes with so many dishes!

INGREDIENTS

- 1 tbsp vegan butter
- 1 onion, finely chopped
- 250g mushrooms, sliced
- ½ tsp salt
- ¼ tsp black pepper
- 1 clove garlic, finely chopped
- 150ml vegan dry white wine
- 150ml vegan cream
- 1 tsp lemon juice
- 1 tsp syrup (eg maple or agave) or brown sugar (optional)
- 1 tbsp parsley, stalks removed and finely chopped

INSTRUCTIONS

1. Fry the onion in the vegan butter until soft.
2. Add the mushrooms, salt and pepper and cook until soft but they haven't released their juices.
3. Add the garlic and fry for a further 2 minutes.
4. Pour the white wine into the pan, bring to the boil and then simmer down until the liquid has reduced by half.
5. Stir through the vegan cream, lemon juice and syrup and heat for a further couple of minutes or until reduced down to your desired consistency.
6. Top with the fresh parsley.

ROASTED RED PEPPER & WALNUT DIP

LEVEL: EASY | PREP TIME: 10 MINUTES | COOK TIME: 25 MINUTES | SERVES: 4-6

This Levantine-inspired dip, also known as muhammara, has everything you could possibly want. It is smoky, spicy, sweet, rich and delicious – serve it with drinks and nibbles as a tasty alternative to hummus.

INGREDIENTS

For a quicker version, see the tip box

- **6 red peppers, deseeded and quartered**
- **6 cloves garlic, peeled**
- **85g walnuts or cashews, roasted (see page 178)**
- **1 tsp cumin seeds, toasted or 1 tsp ground cumin**
- **1 tsp smoked paprika**
- **Pinch of cayenne pepper or chilli flakes**
- **3 tbsp breadcrumbs**
- **3 tbsp pomegranate molasses**
- **1 tbsp lemon juice**
- **2 tbsp olive oil**
- **50ml water**
- **½ tsp salt**
- **¼ tsp black pepper**

INSTRUCTIONS

1. Preheat the oven to 220°C/430°F/Gas Mark 7.
2. Using a large baking tray, evenly spread the peppers then drizzle with olive oil and a sprinkling of salt.
3. Cook for 15 minutes before turning and adding the garlic cloves to the tray.
4. Bake for another 10 minutes or until the peppers are cooked and the skin has started to blacken. Make sure the garlic cloves don't burn so remove them if they are getting too much colour!
5. Remove from the oven and then place in a food processor with all the other ingredients and blend until you have a rough paste or until very smooth if you prefer.

SERVING SUGGESTIONS

—

As a pizza sauce, as an alternative to hummus, bread sticks, dips, falafel, flatbread, mezze, Middle Eastern dishes, pasta, pitta bread, pitta chips, potato chips, raw vegetable sticks, roasted or steamed vegetables, sandwiches, steamed or roasted vegetables, tagines, tortilla chips

TIP

—

For a quicker version, use 6 roasted red peppers from a jar, fry the garlic for 2 minutes (finely chopped this time), use uncooked walnuts or toast them instead of roasting (see page 178) and then blend with all the other ingredients until you get your desired consistency.

PEA, MINT, LENTIL & SUNDRIED TOMATO DIP

LEVEL: EASY | PREP TIME: 10 MINUTES | COOK TIME: 5 MINUTES | SERVES: 4-6

This is one of our favourite dips of all time! Protein-packed and full of fresh flavours, we're really onto something here!

SERVING SUGGESTIONS

—

As an alternative to hummus, burgers, falafel, flatbread, fritters, mezze, pasta, potato chips, raw vegetable sticks, salads, sandwiches, tagines, tortilla chips, wraps

INGREDIENTS

- 200g frozen peas, cooked and cooled
- 150g pre-cooked green lentils (use tinned or from a packet for speed), drained and rinsed
- 70g sundried tomatoes from a jar, drained
- 50g tahini
- 20g fresh basil, stalks removed
- 30g fresh mint, stalks removed
- 3 tbsp lemon juice
- 2 cloves garlic, crushed
- 1 tsp white wine vinegar
- 1 tsp red wine vinegar
- 2 tsp syrup (eg maple or agave)
- ½ tsp salt
- Pinch of black pepper

INSTRUCTIONS

1. Blend all the ingredients until very smooth.
2. Taste the mixture and if necessary add a little more salt, to taste.

5-MINUTE TOASTED MIXED SEEDS

LEVEL: EASY | PREP TIME: 3 MINUTES | COOK TIME: 5-10 MINUTES | SERVES: 4

This is the quickest (and tastiest) way we've found of adding a delicious mix of crunch, texture and all the nutrients seeds have to offer, to a wide variety of dishes. You can also enjoy them as a (very moreish) snack or treat!

INGREDIENTS

SAUCE
- **1 tbsp soy sauce**
- **1 tsp syrup (eg maple or agave)**
- **1 tsp sriracha or a pinch of cayenne pepper, paprika or smoked paprika**

SEEDS
- **100g mixed seeds (eg pumpkin, sunflower, sesame)**

INSTRUCTIONS

SAUCE
1. Stir all the ingredients together in a mug or small bowl. Set aside.

SEEDS
1. Place the seeds in a large frying pan in a single layer without oil.
2. Cook on a medium heat until the seeds start to pop, around 3-5 minutes. Once they start to pop, shake the pan and then heat for a couple more minutes. Make sure the seeds are not burning or browning too quickly. If they are, turn down the heat a little.
3. Take them off the heat and pour over the sauce. Immediately stir the sauce through as the seeds absorb the liquid very quickly.
4. Leave the seeds to dry and cool. They may be a bit sticky to begin with but they will firm up as they cool.
5. Store them in an airtight container at room temperature and keep them for up to 3 weeks.

SERVING SUGGESTIONS

—

Avocado on toast, Buddha bowls, curries, grain bowls, pasta, poke bowls, salads, sandwiches, scrambled tofu, soups, stir-fries, tagines

TIP

—

For a plainer version, take out the sriracha and the syrup and just use the soy sauce.

NUTTY HEAVEN - A GUIDE TO TOASTING & ROASTING NUTS

Try roasting or toasting your nuts! It draws the natural oils to the surface and will add a lovely flavour, colour and texture to your dishes (oh – and protein!). Also sprinkle on top of curries, soups and salads for a bit of extra crunch or enjoy as a delicious snack. You can toast your nuts in a frying pan on the hob or roast them in the oven. Cooking them in the oven roasts them most evenly but toasting them on the hob is quicker! Here's how...

Nut	Toasting (use a frying pan without oil on a medium heat. Heat the pan a little first before adding the nuts)	Roasting (single layer on a baking tray in the oven without oil)	What to sprinkle them over
CASHEWS	**Time: 3-5 minutes or until golden and fragrant, stirring or shaking the pan frequently**	**Oven temperature: 180°C/350°F/ Gas Mark 4** **Time: 8-12 minutes or until golden** **Shake the tray halfway through cooking**	**Curries, Indian dishes, roasted or steamed vegetables, salads, soups, stews, stir-fries, Thai and South East Asian dishes, tofu dishes**
FLAKED ALMONDS	**Time: 2-5 minutes or until golden and fragrant, stirring or shaking the pan frequently**	**Oven temperature: 160°C/325°F/ Gas Mark 3** **Time: 6-8 minutes or until lightly golden** **Shake the tray halfway through cooking**	**Cakes and desserts, ice cream, Middle Eastern dishes, muffins, overnight oats, pancakes, porridge, roasted or steamed vegetables, salads, smoothie bowls, soups, tagines, tarts**
HAZELNUTS	**Time: 5-10 minutes or until golden and fragrant, stirring or shaking the pan frequently**	**Oven temperature: 180°C/350°F/ Gas Mark 4** **Time: 7-10 minutes or until golden** **Shake the tray halfway through cooking**	**Cakes and desserts, chocolate, dips, ice cream, pesto, pizza, roasted or steamed vegetables, salads, soups, stews, stuffed vegetables, vegan mac and cheese**
MACADAMIAS	**Time: 5-10 minutes or until golden and fragrant, stirring or shaking the pan frequently**	**Oven temperature: 120°C/250°F/ Gas Mark ½** **Time: 8-10 minutes or until golden** **Shake the tray halfway through cooking**	**Cakes and desserts, curries, ice cream, pancakes, roasted or steamed vegetables, salads, soups, stews**

PEANUTS	Time: 5-10 minutes or until golden and fragrant, stirring or shaking the pan frequently	Oven temperature: 180°C/350°F/Gas Mark 4. Time: 10-15 minutes or until golden Shake the tray halfway through cooking	Chocolate, desserts, roasted or steamed vegetables, salads, sandwiches, soups, stews, stir-fries, Sub-Saharan African dishes, Thai and South East Asian dishes, tofu dishes, wraps
PECANS	Time: 3-5 minutes or until golden and fragrant, stirring or shaking the pan frequently	Oven temperature: 180°C/350°F/Gas Mark 4. Time: 5-10 minutes or until golden Shake the tray halfway through cooking	Cakes and desserts, cereal, fruit salad, ice cream, Mexican dishes, overnight oats, pancakes, porridge, roasted or steamed vegetables, salads, smoothie bowls, soups, vegan cheese and crackers
PINE NUTS	Time: 2-5 minutes or until golden and fragrant, stirring or shaking the pan frequently	Oven temperature: 180°C/350°F/Gas Mark 4. Time: 5-7 minutes or until golden Shake the tray halfway through cooking	Gnocchi, hummus and dips, Mediterranean dishes, Middle Eastern dishes, pasta, pesto, quiches, risotto, roasted or steamed vegetables, salads, soups, stews, stuffed vegetables, tagines, tarts
PISTACHIOS	Time: 3-5 minutes or until golden and fragrant, stirring or shaking the pan frequently	Oven temperature: 180°C/350°F/Gas Mark 4 Time: 8-10 minutes or until golden Shake the tray halfway through cooking	Dips, ice cream, Mediterranean dishes, Middle Eastern dishes, pasta, risottos, roasted or steamed vegetables, salads, tagines, tarts
WALNUTS	Time: 2-5 minutes or until golden and fragrant, stirring or shaking the pan frequently	Oven temperature: 180°C/350°F/Gas Mark 4 Time: 7-10 minutes or until golden Shake the tray halfway through cooking	Cereal, fruit salad, overnight oats, pasta, porridge, risottos, salads, smoothie bowls, soups, stews, stuffed vegetables, tarts, vegan cheese and crackers
WHOLE ALMONDS	Time: 3-5 minutes or until golden and fragrant, stirring or shaking the pan frequently	Oven temperature: 160°C/325°F/Gas Mark 3. Time: 8-12 minutes or until golden Shake the tray halfway through cooking	Cereal, Middle Eastern dishes, overnight oats, porridge, roasted or steamed vegetables, salads, smoothie bowls, tagines

CAKES, BAKES AND DESSERTS

CLASSIC VICTORIA SPONGE

LEVEL: EASY | PREP TIME: 30 MINUTES | COOK TIME: 35 MINUTES | SERVES: 10

We've received lovely feedback about this Victoria sponge recipe – and we're told it works consistently every time. You'll achieve a big fluffy rise without losing moisture and you can have lots of fun with the icing and strawberries – enjoy this classic!

INGREDIENTS

WET INGREDIENTS
- **400ml unsweetened soya or almond milk**
- **150ml neutral oil (eg rapeseed)**
- **1 tbsp vanilla extract**
- **1 tbsp cider vinegar**

DRY INGREDIENTS
- **400g self-raising flour**
- **275g golden caster sugar**
- **2 tsp baking powder**
- **½ tsp salt**

VEGAN BUTTER ICING
- **100g vegan butter, chilled**
- **1 tbsp vanilla extract**
- **1 tbsp unsweetened plant milk (use a tiny amount extra bit by bit, if needed)**
- **500g vegan icing sugar, sieved**

OTHER
- **Layer of jam – use as much as you like**
- **Strawberries for decoration (optional)**

INSTRUCTIONS

1. Preheat the oven to 180°C/350°F/Gas Mark 4.

2. Grease and line 2 round cake tins (20cm diameter approx.).

WET INGREDIENTS

1. In a large jug, stir together all the wet ingredients and then leave for a few minutes.

DRY INGREDIENTS

1. In a large mixing bowl, thoroughly combine all the dry ingredients.

2. Pour the wet ingredients into the bowl of dry ingredients and stir until combined (but don't over-stir).

3. Evenly distribute the cake mixture between the 2 tins. Tap the tins on the side of the work surface (this stops the raising agents from working too quickly).

4. Place them in the oven for 20-35 minutes or until lightly golden and a knife/skewer comes out clean. Leave to cool completely.

VEGAN BUTTER ICING

1. Using a balloon whisk, electric hand whisk, stand mixer or food processor, mix all the ingredients together until smooth and firm(ish). Transfer to the fridge to chill.

ASSEMBLY

1. Once cooled, remove one of the sponges from the tin and spread half the vegan butter icing over the top.

2. Add a layer of jam on top of the vegan butter icing then place the other half of the cake on top.

3. Spread the other half of the vegan butter icing over the top of the cake and decorate with a dusting of icing sugar and strawberries (optional).

GOOEY CHOCOLATE FUDGE CAKE

LEVEL: EASY | PREP TIME: 15 MINUTES | COOK TIME: 25 MINUTES | SERVES: 10

Chocolate heaven – tick. Squidgy, fudgy deliciousness – tick. Crowd-pleaser – tick. Good-looking – tick... need we go on?!

INGREDIENTS

WET INGREDIENTS
- 385ml unsweetened soya or almond milk
- 1 tbsp cider vinegar
- 125ml neutral oil (eg rapeseed)
- 1 tbsp vanilla extract
- 3 tbsp golden syrup

DRY INGREDIENTS
- 300g self-raising flour
- 100g cocoa powder
- 225g golden caster sugar
- 2 tsp baking powder
- 1 tsp salt

VEGAN BUTTER ICING
- 100g vegan butter, chilled
- 1 tbsp vanilla extract
- 1 tbsp unsweetened plant milk (use a tiny amount extra bit by bit, if needed)
- 450g icing sugar, sieved
- 50g cocoa powder, sieved

Optional toppings: fresh berries, vegan chocolate buttons or chips, vegan chocolate sauce, vegan white and dark chocolate shavings

INSTRUCTIONS

1. Preheat the oven to 180°C/350°F/Gas Mark 4.

2. Grease and line 2 round cake tins (approx. 20cm diameter).

WET INGREDIENTS

1. In a large jug, thoroughly whisk all the wet ingredients together and set aside for 10 minutes.

DRY INGREDIENTS

1. In a large bowl, stir all the dry ingredients together.

2. Pour the wet ingredients into the bowl of dry ingredients and stir until combined (but don't over-stir).

3. Evenly distribute the cake mixture between the 2 tins. Tap the tins on the side of the work surface (this stops the raising agents from working too quickly).

4. Place them in the oven for 20-25 minutes or until a knife/skewer comes out clean. Leave to cool completely.

VEGAN BUTTER ICING

1. Using a balloon whisk, electric hand whisk, stand mixer or food processor, mix all the ingredients together until smooth and firm(ish). Transfer to the fridge to chill.

ASSEMBLY

1. Remove one of the sponges from the tin and spread about a third of the butter icing over the top. Place the other half of the cake on top.

2. Spread another third of the icing over the top of the cake.

3. Spread the remaining third of the icing around the sides of the cake, ideally using a palette knife.

4. Decorate with your choice of optional toppings.

MOIST & EASY CARROT CAKE

LEVEL: EASY | PREP TIME: 15 MINUTES | COOK TIME: 25 MINUTES | SERVES: 10

We couldn't make a cookbook without including a classic carrot cake recipe. Viva!'s Managing Director tried it and announced it was the best cake she'd ever eaten! It's really simple to make (please don't tell her!) and the warming spices of cinnamon, ginger and nutmeg really make it. If you're feeling extra indulgent, try drizzling a slice with maple syrup or serve with vegan ice cream.

INGREDIENTS

WET INGREDIENTS
- 2 flax eggs (mix 2 tbsp ground flaxseed with 6 tbsp water and set aside)
- 400ml unsweetened soya or almond milk
- 1 tbsp cider vinegar
- 160ml neutral oil (eg rapeseed)
- 250g grated carrot (roughly 4 medium-sized carrots)

DRY INGREDIENTS
- 400g self-raising flour
- 2 tsp baking powder
- 300g soft brown sugar (we like light muscovado)
- ½ tsp salt
- 1½ tsp ground cinnamon
- 1 tsp ground ginger
- ¼ tsp ground or fresh nutmeg, grated
- ¼ tsp ground cloves
- 125g pecans, roughly chopped (optional), plus a few more for decoration

ICING
- 110g vegan butter, chilled
- 225g vegan cream cheese, chilled
- 2 tsp lemon juice
- 600g vegan icing sugar, sieved
- 2 tsp vanilla extract or paste

INSTRUCTIONS

1. Preheat the oven to 180°C/350°F/Gas Mark 4.
2. Grease and line 2 round cake tins (20cm diameter approx.).

WET INGREDIENTS
1. In a large jug, mix up the soya or almond milk with the cider vinegar and set aside for 5 minutes.
2. Add all of the other wet ingredients to the jug, including the flax eggs and carrots, and mix well.

DRY INGREDIENTS
1. Combine all the dry ingredients together thoroughly in a large mixing bowl. Set aside.
2. Add the wet ingredients to the bowl of dry ingredients and stir through until combined (don't over-stir).
3. Immediately pour the mixture evenly into the 2 lined cake tins. Give each tin a tap on the work surface (this stops the raising agents working too quickly) before placing them into the oven.
4. Bake the cakes for 20 minutes then test with a skewer or knife and put back in the oven until the skewer/knife comes out clean. If the cake is starting to brown too quickly then cover it with foil or greaseproof paper. Leave to cool before icing.

ICING
1. Using a balloon whisk, electric hand whisk, stand mixer or food processor, mix all the ingredients together until smooth and firm(ish). Transfer to the fridge to chill.

ASSEMBLY
1. Spread half the icing on one cake, sit the other cake on top, and spread the remaining icing on top.
2. Decorate the top of the cake with whole and chopped pecans. Add a drizzle of maple syrup if you're feeling extra indulgent!

RASPBERRY BAKEWELL CAKE

LEVEL: EASY | PREP TIME: 10 MINUTES | COOK TIME: 35 MINUTES | SERVES: 10

We wanted to combine two of our favourite things to make one extraordinary recipe – Bakewell tart and cake! You'll be surprised how easy it is to make and yet it's full of flavour, moist and bursting with almondy yumminess!

INGREDIENTS

WET INGREDIENTS
- 300ml unsweetened soya or almond milk
- 115ml neutral oil (eg rapeseed)
- ¾ tbsp cider vinegar
- 2 tsp almond extract
- 1 tsp vanilla extract

DRY INGREDIENTS
- 100g ground almonds
- 200g self-raising flour
- 210g golden caster sugar
- 1½ tsp baking powder
- ¼ tsp salt

OTHER
- 225g (approx.) raspberries
- Blobs of raspberry or cherry jam (optional)
- 2 x handfuls (approx.) of vegan white chocolate chips or broken vegan white chocolate chunks (optional)
- 5 tbsp flaked almonds
- Vegan icing sugar for dusting

SERVING SUGGESTIONS
—
Coconut yoghurt, fresh mint, fresh raspberries, vegan crème fraîche

INSTRUCTIONS

WET INGREDIENTS
1. In a large jug, whisk all the ingredients really well and set aside for 10 minutes.

DRY INGREDIENTS
1. Preheat the oven to 180°C/350°F/Gas Mark 4.
2. Line a 23cm (approx.) springform cake tin.
3. In a large mixing bowl, thoroughly combine all the dry ingredients and set aside.
4. Just before you're ready to put the cake into the oven, pour the wet ingredients into the bowl of dry ingredients and thoroughly combine without over-stirring. This is your cake mixture.

OTHER/ASSEMBLY
1. Pour half of the cake mixture into the bottom of the lined cake tin and make sure that it's evenly spread.
2. Place the raspberries over the mixture, making sure they're evenly spaced but don't push them down.
3. Add some blobs of jam over the raspberries. Also evenly add the vegan white chocolate at this stage, if using.
4. Pour over the other half of the cake mixture, covering the layer of raspberries.
5. Evenly sprinkle the flaked almonds over the top of the mixture.
6. Place in the oven and bake for 30-40 minutes depending on your oven. Check after 30 minutes and see if a knife/skewer comes out clean. If not, pop in for another 5-10 minutes until properly cooked.
7. Leave to cool before serving.
8. Dust with icing sugar and serve.

CHOCOLATE TORTE WITH BERRY BURST

LEVEL: NOT TOO TRICKY | PREP TIME: 10 MINUTES | COOK TIME: 20 MINUTES | CHILL TIME: 3 HOURS | SERVES: 10

This divine chocolate torte really does taste as good as it looks. With a crunchy biscuit base, silky chocolate topping and berry burst centre, this is a seriously decadent dessert that your guests will go mad for – trust us!

INGREDIENTS

BASE
- **250g vegan digestive biscuits**
- **120g vegan butter**

RASPBERRY LAYER
- **300g fresh raspberries**
- **75g golden caster sugar**

CHOCOLATE LAYER
- **250g vegan dark chocolate (70% cocoa solids)**
- **250g vegan milk chocolate**
- **100g golden caster sugar**
- **1 tsp salt**
- **130ml sweetened plant milk**
- **75ml olive oil**
- **100ml Amaretto (just be aware this contains nuts. If you want to leave out the alcohol then substitute this with 100ml extra plant milk)**
- **2 tsp vanilla extract**

SERVING SUGGESTIONS
—
Chopped nuts, dusting of cocoa powder, freeze-dried raspberries, fresh berries, fresh mint, raspberry coulis, vegan cream or crème fraîche, vegan ice cream

INSTRUCTIONS

1. Preheat the oven to 180°C/350°F/Gas Mark 4.
2. Grease a springform cake tin (20-25cm diameter approx.).

BASE
1. Thoroughly blend the biscuits in a food processor or bash them with a rolling pin until fine and then pour them into a large mixing bowl.
2. Gently melt the butter in a small saucepan on a low heat until fully melted. Combine thoroughly with the blended digestives.
3. Empty the mixture into the bottom of the greased cake tin and press down firmly and evenly. Place in the oven for 5-10 minutes until slightly golden. Set aside to cool.

RASPBERRY LAYER
1. In a medium saucepan, mix the raspberries and sugar together on a medium heat. Simmer for 10 minutes or until reduced down (it's really important to reduce it down to a sticky, jammy consistency and not too runny). Set aside to cool.

CHOCOLATE LAYER
1. Melt the chocolate, sugar and salt together using a double boiler/bain marie (a glass or ceramic bowl that fits on a saucepan of simmering water but doesn't touch the bottom), stirring frequently, to make sure the sugar is thoroughly dissolved (don't remove from the heat until the sugar is fully dissolved).
2. Remove from the heat and cool slightly before adding the other ingredients.
3. Stir in the plant milk, olive oil, Amaretto and vanilla extract and mix until fully combined and smooth. Once combined, don't over-stir.
4. Pour half the chocolate mixture over the base, then evenly spread over the raspberry layer but leave about 1cm around the edge. Pour the other half of the chocolate mix over the top to cover the raspberry layer and give the tin a little tap to level out the top.
5. Place in the fridge and leave to chill for a minimum of 3 hours.
6. Decorate with fresh rasberries or your choice of toppings.

STRAWBERRY & CREAM CUPCAKES

LEVEL: NOT TOO TRICKY | PREP TIME: 15 MINUTES | COOK TIME: 25 MINUTES | SERVES: 10

Kids and adults will have lots of fun creating these colourful cupcakes! Enjoy a light, fluffy sponge, a creamy butter icing and a variety of decorations to get imaginative with.

INGREDIENTS

WET INGREDIENTS
- 100ml neutral oil (eg rapeseed)
- 2 tsp vanilla extract
- 250ml unsweetened soya or almond milk
- 1½ tsp cider vinegar

DRY INGREDIENTS
- 250g self-raising flour
- 250g caster sugar
- ½ tsp bicarbonate of soda
- ½ tsp baking powder

ICING
- 150g vegan butter, chilled
- 750g icing sugar, sieved
- 1 tbsp unsweetened plant milk (add tiny bit by bit if extra is needed)
- 1½ tbsp vanilla extract
- A few drops of vegan red food colouring

Optional decoration: edible flowers, freeze-dried raspberries/strawberries, fresh strawberries, mixed nuts, vegan strawberry sauce, vegan white chocolate

INSTRUCTIONS

1. Preheat the oven to 180°C/350°F/Gas Mark 4.
2. Line a muffin tray with muffin cases or cupcake cases. This recipe will make 10 large cupcakes or 15-20 smaller ones.

WET INGREDIENTS

1. In a large jug, thoroughly whisk together all the wet ingredients and set aside for 10 minutes.

DRY INGREDIENTS

1. In a large mixing bowl, thoroughly combine all the dry ingredients.
2. Pour the wet ingredients into the dry ingredients and combine but don't overstir.
3. Tap the bowl onto the work surface to stop the raising agents working too quickly.
4. Fill the cupcake cases to three-quarters full and tap the tray again.
5. Place the tray in the oven and bake for 15-25 minutes depending on the size of the cupcake. They need to be slightly golden on the surface.
6. Remove from the oven and leave to cool thoroughly before icing.

ICING

1. Using a balloon whisk, electric hand whisk, stand mixer or food processor, mix together the vegan butter, icing sugar and plant milk.
2. You can add more icing sugar or plant milk if the icing gets too wet or too dry.
3. Separate the icing into 2 and place it in 2 different bowls.
4. Add a couple of drops of red food colouring to one of the bowls of icing until you get your desired colour.
5. Add your favourite cupcake nozzle to a piping bag (these can be bought from supermarkets, online and kitchen shops) and then fill with one colour of the icing.
6. Ice half the cakes with the white icing and half with the pink icing.
7. Decorate with the optional decorations.

NO-BAKE MILLIONAIRE'S SHORTBREAD

LEVEL: NOT TOO TRICKY | PREP TIME: 20 MINUTES | CHILL TIME: 3 HOURS | SERVES: 10-15

We tried this on some of our long-term supporters and they said it is one of the nicest things they've ever eaten! Considering how healthy this recipe is it really shouldn't taste this good – but we're delighted it does!

INGREDIENTS

BASE
- **150g unsalted cashew nuts**
- **50g rolled oats**
- **4 Medjool dates, pitted**
- **50g coconut oil, melted (use odourless/culinary if you don't want a coconutty taste)**

CARAMEL LAYER
- **300g Medjool dates, pitted**
- **80g nut butter (we like almond butter)**
- **5 tbsp unsweetened plant milk**
- **1 tsp vanilla extract**
- **1 tsp salt**
- **2 tbsp syrup (eg maple or agave)**

CHOCOLATE TOPPING
- **60g coconut oil (use odourless/culinary if you don't want a coconutty taste)**
- **40g cocoa powder or raw cacao powder**
- **1 tsp vanilla extract**
- **2 tbsp syrup (eg maple or agave)**
- **Pinch of salt**

INSTRUCTIONS

BASE
1. Grease and line a 20cm square cake tin.
2. Using a food processor, blitz the nuts and oats to crumbs. Add the dates and melted coconut oil and blend again. Spoon the mixture evenly into the tin, covering the entire base and press down. Chill in the freezer while you make the filling.

CARAMEL LAYER
1. Using a food processor or high-speed blender, blend all the ingredients until smooth. Spread this layer evenly over the base and return to the freezer for a minimum of 30 minutes.

CHOCOLATE TOPPING
1. In a small saucepan, melt the coconut oil on a low heat. Add all the other ingredients to the pan and heat for a few minutes until combined, stirring frequently. Pour the chocolate layer over the caramel then place in the fridge to set for 2 hours minimum.
2. Cut into squares, share and enjoy!

BERRY CRUMBLE SLICES

LEVEL: EASY | PREP TIME: 15 MINUTES | COOK TIME: 35 MINUTES | SERVES: 15

You can't go wrong with a good old berry crumble so how about changing it up and turning it into easy-to-carry slices for portable goodies galore?!

INGREDIENTS

BASE/CRUMBLE
- **300g plain flour**
- **150g sugar (brown sugar tastes best)**
- **¾ tsp baking powder**
- **¾ tsp ground cinnamon**
- **200g vegan butter, chilled**

BLUEBERRY FILLING
- **350g blueberries (fresh or frozen, defrosted)**
- **Zest of 1 lemon, finely chopped**
- **1½ tbsp lemon juice**
- **2 tsp cornflour**
- **2½ tbsp sugar**
- **Pinch of salt**
- **1½ tsp vanilla extract or paste**

INSTRUCTIONS

1. Preheat the oven to 180°C/350°F/Gas Mark 4.

2. Line a 20cm square tin with greaseproof paper.

BASE/CRUMBLE

1. In a large bowl, mix all the ingredients together apart from the butter.

2. Add the butter and work it in thoroughly with your hands until you have a fine crumble.

3. Set aside 160g of the crumble for the topping and press the rest of the crumble mix into the baking tin.

4. Place it in the oven for 10 minutes then leave it to cool for 5-10 minutes before adding the blueberry filling.

BLUEBERRY FILLING/ASSEMBLY

1. Mix all the filling ingredients together in a large bowl.

2. Pour the blueberry filling onto the base, making sure it's evenly spread (keep the blueberries whole).

3. Next, sprinkle the remaining crumble topping evenly over the filling.

4. Place in the oven for 25-30 minutes (or until golden on the top) but check after 20 minutes that it's not browning too quickly. If it browns too quickly then cover with foil or greaseproof paper.

5. Remove from the oven and enjoy warm or cold.

SPEEDY ROCKY ROAD

LEVEL: EASY | PREP TIME: 20 MINUTES | SETTING TIME: 2 HOURS | SERVES: 15

If you like desserts which are unbelievably simple to make but seriously impress friends and family, then this one's for you! You can take out any of the filling options and change them for something else if you fancy – it's a fun one to make for adults and kids alike!

INGREDIENTS

- 150g vegan dark chocolate (70% cocoa solids)
- 150g vegan milk chocolate
- 125g vegan butter
- 3 tbsp golden syrup
- ¼ tsp salt
- 200g vegan digestives or rich tea biscuits
- 100g vegan mini marshmallows
- 50g vegan puffed rice cereal (optional)
- 50g raisins, dried cranberries or chopped apricots
- 2 tbsp icing sugar, sieved or 30g vegan white chocolate, melted (for decoration)

INSTRUCTIONS

1. Grease and line a 20cm square brownie tin.
2. In a large saucepan, melt the vegan chocolate, vegan butter, golden syrup and salt on a low heat.
3. Seal the 200g biscuits in a freezer bag and bash them into pieces. It's good to have a mixture of biscuit crumbs, smaller and larger pieces.
4. Add the biscuits, vegan marshmallows, raisins and vegan puffed rice (or alternative fillings) to the melted chocolate mixture and stir through until completely covered.
5. Empty the mixture into the lined baking tin, spreading evenly.
6. Pop it in the fridge and chill for 2 hours, minimum.
7. To decorate, dust with icing sugar or drizzle with melted vegan white chocolate.
8. Cut into evenly-sized squares according to how big you would like them and enjoy!

TIP
—
For a bit of variety try changing the fillings for pistachios or other nuts, popcorn, seasonal treats, eg Easter goodies, vegan honeycomb etc.

SIMPLE STRAWBERRY GALETTE WITH VEGAN WHIPPED CREAM

LEVEL: EASY | PREP TIME: 10 MINUTES | COOK TIME: 20 MINUTES | CHILL TIME: 3 HOURS (THIS STAGE DOESN'T APPLY IF YOU USE THE QUICK CREAM OPTION) | SERVES: 6

This is Juliet Gellatley's favourite dessert! It's very simple to make but looks like a showstopper, delighting adults and kids alike!

INGREDIENTS

CREAM
Use this cream recipe any time you need a whipped cream – just remove the lemon zest and reduce the icing sugar if you don't want it too sweet. It pipes well too.

- **300g unsweetened soya, oat or cashew milk (you can use sweetened but reduce the icing sugar by 50g)**
- **250g odourless/culinary coconut oil (you can use regular if you want a coconutty taste), melted**
- **150g icing sugar, sieved**
- **1 tsp vanilla extract**
- **Zest of ½ a lemon, finely chopped (optional)**

STRAWBERRIES
- **1kg fresh strawberries, hulled (if you leave them whole they look prettier but halving or quartering them makes them much easier and nicer to eat)**
- **4 tbsp icing sugar, sieved**

PASTRY
- **320g vegan ready-to-use puff pastry sheet**

Optional decoration: chopped nuts, dusting of icing sugar, edible flowers, fresh mint sprigs

INSTRUCTIONS

CREAM
1. Heat the plant milk in the microwave (or on the hob for a little longer) for around 30 seconds to a minute (you want it to be warm but not hot).
2. Pour the heated plant milk and melted coconut oil into a high-speed blender and blend for around 1 minute.
3. Place the mixture in the fridge for a minimum of 3 hours or overnight.
4. Transfer the mixture to a large bowl and use an electric hand whisk or place in the bowl of a stand mixer with whisk attachment. Add the icing sugar and vanilla extract.
5. Whisk the ingredients together on the highest setting. It will take 5-10 minutes to start to thicken – don't give up, it will happen eventually!
6. When stiff peaks form and you have your desired consistency, stop whisking or it will start to curdle.
7. Stir through the lemon zest then place in the fridge until needed.

STRAWBERRIES
1. Liquidise 200g of the hulled strawberries and then push them through a sieve and into a jug to create a smooth paste. Stir in the icing sugar then place in the fridge until needed.
2. Set the remaining strawberries aside until the decoration stage.

PASTRY
1. Preheat the oven to 180°C/350°F/Gas Mark 4.
2. Place the sheet of puff pastry on a baking tray lined with greaseproof paper, prick it with a fork and then pop in the oven for 15 minutes or until golden.
3. Take the sheet out, turn it over, gently press it down to flatten it again and return it to the oven for another 5-10 minutes.
4. Leave to cool for minimum 15 minutes.
5. Spread the cream evenly over the cooled puff pastry sheet, leaving about a couple of centimetres of pastry showing around the edges.
6. Place the fresh strawberries evenly over the layer of cream.
7. Top off with the liquidised strawberry paste and optional decorations.

TIP
—

For a quicker cream option, thoroughly combine 600ml vegan crème fraîche or vegan whippable cream, 150g icing sugr, ½ tbsp lemon juice and zest and 1 tsp vanilla extract.

STICKY TOFFEE PUDDINGS

LEVELS: NOT TOO TRICKY | PREP TIME: 15 MINUTES | COOK TIME: 45 MINUTES | SERVES: 4

There are few things in life as enjoyable as a sticky toffee pudding! Savour our scrumptiously veganised version of this classic British dessert, with a treacly date sponge covered in a delectable toffee sauce – ideally topped with vegan ice cream (we think so anyway)!

INGREDIENTS

DATE MIX
- **110ml water**
- **200ml unsweetened plant milk**
- **200g dates, pitted and chopped into small pieces**

WET INGREDIENTS
- **1 tbsp cider vinegar**
- **2 tbsp unsweetened plant milk**
- **110g vegan butter, very slightly softened (but not liquid!)**
- **1 tsp vanilla extract**

DRY INGREDIENTS
- **200g self-raising flour**
- **½ tsp ground cinnamon**
- **Pinch of ground cloves**
- **60g light muscovado sugar**
- **60g golden caster sugar**
- **95g chopped walnuts (optional)**
- **1 tsp bicarbonate of soda**
- **Pinch of salt**

STICKY TOFFEE SAUCE
- **3 tbsp golden syrup**
- **100g light muscovado sugar**
- **100g golden caster sugar**
- **120ml vegan cream**
- **150g vegan butter**
- **1 tsp vanilla extract**

Optional toppings: dusting of icing sugar, fresh berries, fresh mint

INSTRUCTIONS

1. Preheat the oven to 180°C/350°F/Gas Mark 4.
2. Grease 4 pudding basins (200ml approx.) with vegan spread and place them on a baking tray.

DATE MIX
1. Place the water, plant milk and dates into a medium-sized saucepan and simmer for around 5 minutes or until the dates are soft. Set aside and do not drain off the water/plant milk.

WET INGREDIENTS
1. In a large jug, thoroughly whisk together all the wet ingredients and set aside for 5 minutes.

DRY INGREDIENTS
1. In a large bowl thoroughly combine all the dry ingredients.
2. Pour the date mix and the wet ingredients into the bowl of dry ingredients. Thoroughly combine but don't overstir.
3. Pour the mixture evenly into each pudding basin to around two-thirds full.
4. Place the pudding basins onto a baking tray and then give the tray a tap on a work surface before placing it in the oven (this stops the raising agents working too quickly).
5. Bake in the oven for 25 minutes or until a knife comes out clean.

STICKY TOFFEE SAUCE
1. Make the sauce around 10 minutes before the puddings are due to come out of the oven.
2. Place all the ingredients in a medium-sized saucepan and heat gently on a medium heat, stirring frequently. Simmer for 5 minutes.
3. When the puddings are cooked, tip each one out onto a small dish or a flat-bottomed bowl and pour over the sauce. Serve hot.

SERVING SUGGESTIONS

Vegan cream, vegan crème fraîche, vegan custard, vegan honeycomb, vegan ice cream

FLUFFY CHOCOLATE MOUSSE

LEVEL: NOT TOO TRICKY | PREP TIME: 15 MINUTES | CHILL TIME: 4-6 HOURS | SERVES: 6

Viva!'s Head of Research and fellow-foodie, Dr Justine Butler, has been boldly going to new frontiers of aquafaba cooking! Her stunning and simple chocolate mousse has the fluffy mouthfeel of the stuff made with eggs – but, of course, it's all completely and deliciously vegan.

INGREDIENTS

- **200g vegan dark chocolate**
- **90g coconut cream (don't confuse this with creamed coconut)**
- **160ml aquafaba (the thick strained liquid from a tin of chickpeas. Use the whole chickpeas in another dish, eg hummus or a curry)**
- **115g caster sugar**
- **1 tsp vanilla extract**
- **Pinch of salt**

Optional toppings: boozy berries, fresh berries, fresh mint, raspberry coulis, vegan chocolate sauce, vegan chocolate shavings or chocolate chips (white or dark), vegan crème fraîche, vegan honeycomb, vegan squirty cream

INSTRUCTIONS

1. Melt the chocolate and coconut cream together in a glass bowl over a pan of boiling water.
2. Remove from the heat and stand the bowl on the side to cool. If the chocolate splits and you get dark clumpy chocolate and clear fat, add a small amount of water (a few teaspoonfuls) and stir – it will go creamy again. Set aside.
3. Whisk the aquafaba in a clean glass bowl with an electric hand whisk or stand mixer until stiff peaks form (this might take a bit of time – don't give up!).
4. Slowly add the caster sugar, whisking all the time.
5. When the chocolate has cooled quite a bit, gently fold it into the aquafaba with the vanilla extract and salt. Stir gently – you don't want it to collapse.
6. Transfer into glasses, jars or small coffee cups and chill in the fridge for at least 4-6 hours.

TIP

—

For a stiffer whip and more bubbles in your mousse, reduce the aquafaba down to 100ml (approx.) by simmering on a medium heat. Cool before using.

SERVING SUGGESTIONS

—

Dusting of icing sugar, edible flowers, freeze-dried raspberries, fresh berries, fresh mint, lemon zest, vegan chocolate shavings, vegan crème fraîche, vegan ice cream, vegan squirty cream

WHITE CHOCOLATE & RASPBERRY CHEESECAKE

**LEVEL: NOT TOO TRICKY | PREP TIME: 20 MINUTES | COOK TIME: 1 HOUR AND 30 MINUTES
SETTING TIME: OVERNIGHT | SERVES: 10-12**

There's a little bit more faff involved with this recipe but don't let that put you off! Everyone who has tried it has said it's to die for and they can't tell it apart from the non-vegan version – prepare to be wowed!

INGREDIENTS

BASE
- **400g vegan digestive biscuits**
- **170g vegan butter**

CAKE
- **100g ground almonds**
- **500g vegan cream cheese**
- **1 x 400ml tin coconut milk**
- **150g caster sugar**
- **6 tbsp plain flour, sieved**
- **4 tbsp cornflour**
- **1-2 tsp lemon juice (fresh or bottled)**
- **¼ tsp salt**
- **1-2 tsp vanilla paste or extract**
- **1 tbsp odourless/culinary coconut oil, melted (you can use regular if you don't mind a coconutty taste)**
- **150g vegan white chocolate**
- **100g raspberries**

TOPPING
- **170g raspberries**
- **2 tbsp raspberry jam**
- **300g vegan icing sugar, sieved**
- **Selection of mixed berries and fresh mint for decoration (optional)**

INSTRUCTIONS

BASE

1. Preheat the oven to 150°C/300°F/Gas Mark 2.

2. Grease a 20cm (approx.), deep springform cake tin.

3. Blend the biscuits until fine crumbs or put in a clean tea towel and bash with a rolling pin.

4. Gently melt the butter then combine thoroughly with the biscuit crumbs in a large mixing bowl.

5. Empty the mixture into the greased cake tin and evenly distribute it, pushing down firmly. Place in the fridge.

CAKE

1. Thoroughly blend the ground almonds, vegan cream cheese, coconut milk, sugar, flour, cornflour, lemon juice, salt, vanilla paste and melted coconut oil until smooth.

2. Melt the white chocolate using a double boiler/bain marie (a glass or ceramic bowl that fits on a saucepan of simmering water but doesn't touch the bottom) and then pour immediately into the cake mix and blend again.

3. Take the base out of the fridge and pour the cake mix evenly over the base.

4. Push the rasberries into the mixture until they are fully submerged.

5. Fill a deep baking tray with water (around 3cm). Make sure the bottom of the tin is really securely covered with foil before placing it into the water.

6. Also cover the top of the cake with foil.

7. Place the tray with the cake into the preheated oven and bake for 1 hour 30 minutes.

8. When the cake is ready (it might be a bit wobbly in the middle and this is fine, it will set), take it out of the oven and leave it to cool for an hour before putting it into the fridge to set overnight.

TOPPING

1. Heat the raspberries and the jam on a low heat for 5 minutes until combined and smooth. Squish the raspberries against the side of the pan with a wooden spoon if they still remain whole.

2. Add the sieved icing sugar to the pan and heat until fully dissolved.

3. Pass the sauce through a sieve and then pour it on the top of the cake until fully covered. Top with berries and set in the fridge for another hour.

EASY-PEASY SODA BREAD

LEVEL: EASY | PREP TIME: 10 MINUTES | COOK TIME: 30 MINUTES | SERVES: 10

We weren't going to include any bread recipes in the cookbook but we just couldn't resist this one! It's so straightforward, tasty and incredibly rewarding to make. It uses bicarbonate of soda as the leavening agent so there's no proving time. The end result looks like it's come from an artisan bakery – enjoy!

INGREDIENTS

- 250g plain wholemeal flour
- 250g plain white flour
- 1 tsp bicarbonate of soda
- 1 tsp salt
- 420ml unsweetened plant milk
- Juice of 1 lime
- Extra flour for dusting

INSTRUCTIONS

1. Preheat the oven to 200°C/400°F/Gas Mark 6.
2. In a large bowl, mix together the 2 types of flour, bicarbonate of soda and salt.
3. Add the milk and lime juice and mix until a sticky dough forms.
4. Lightly flour a work surface and tip the dough onto it.
5. Gently roll and fold the dough a couple of times to bring the mixture together. Do not knead. Sprinkle with a little more flour if necessary to make a smooth dough.
6. Shape the dough into a ball. Flatten the ball a little bit, gently with your hand. Score the dough with a deep cross dividing it into quarters. Dust the bread with flour.
7. Place onto a baking tray lined with greaseproof paper and bake for 30 minutes. The loaf should be golden-brown.
8. Leave to cool on a wire rack. Best eaten fresh but the loaf will last for a few days in an airtight container.

SNACKS

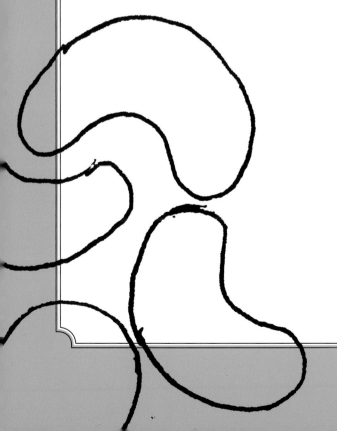

EASIEST ENERGY BALLS

LEVEL: EASY | PREP TIME: 5 MINUTES | COOK TIME: 10 MINUTES | SERVES: 10

The thing that everybody loves about these energy balls is that they are the easiest in the world to make! Full of healthy, protein-packed yumminess, they can be made in just five minutes. Enjoy them fresh throughout the week or freeze them for another time. Perfect post-workout, as a breakfast on the go or as a between-meals snack.

INGREDIENTS

- **1 cup of Brazil nuts**
- **1½ cups of raisins or dates, pitted**
- **1 cup of desiccated coconut plus extra for the coating**
- **1 tbsp raw cacao or cocoa powder (optional)**
- **Pinch of salt (optional)**

Note: if you don't have measuring cups, use a large mug for this recipe as it doesn't need to be precise.

INSTRUCTIONS

1. Blend all the ingredients together using a high-speed blender or food processor.
2. Form into small balls and then dip into a bowl of desiccated coconut to coat.
3. Keep the energy balls in the fridge for up to 7 days in an airtight container or freeze them.

SOFT & CHEWY CEREAL BARS

**LEVEL: EASY | PREP TIME: 5 MINUTES | COOK TIME: 5 MINUTES
CHILL TIME: 30 MINUTES (MINIMUM) | SERVES: 10**

These cereal bars are great for lunchboxes, breakfast on the go or as a healthy treat any time of day! For a budget version try using peanuts instead of hazelnuts, walnuts or pecans, sunflower seeds and raisins instead of goji and cranberries and use a basic peanut butter – just as delicious and won't break the bank!

INGREDIENTS

DRY INGREDIENTS
- 65g hazelnuts, walnuts or pecans (use pre-chopped, mixed nuts if short of time), chopped and ideally toasted or roasted (see page 178)
- 40g vegan puffed rice cereal
- 140g rolled oats
- 1 tsp ground cinnamon
- 35g pumpkin seeds
- 25g cacao nibs
- 40g goji berries
- 20g dried cranberries
- ¼ tsp salt

WET INGREDIENTS
- 110ml syrup (eg maple or agave)
- 70g nut butter of your choice
- 50g coconut oil (use odourless/culinary if you don't want a coconutty taste)
- 1 tsp vanilla extract

INSTRUCTIONS

1. Line a 20cm square cake tin with greaseproof paper, making sure there's a good overhang so you can pull the mixture out easily.

DRY INGREDIENTS
1. Thoroughly combine all the dry ingredients in a large mixing bowl and set aside.

WET INGREDIENTS
1. In a small pan heat the syrup, nut butter and coconut oil on a gentle heat for around 5 minutes.

2. Give it a good stir and add the vanilla extract. Pour the mixture over the dry ingredients until thoroughly combined and sticking together.

ASSEMBLY
1. Pour the mixture into the lined tin and press it down firmly.

2. Chill for 2 hours or overnight (or freeze for 30 minutes) before cutting into 10 bars.

3. Keep the bars in the fridge for up to 7 days in an airtight container or freeze them.

COOKIE DOUGH PROTEIN BITES

LEVEL: EASY | PREP TIME: 5 MINUTES | CHILL TIME: 2 HOURS | SERVES: 10

These moreish little bites make for the perfect protein-packed snack every time! Enjoy them post-workout, for a mid-morning munch or even as an after-dinner treat... who said healthy couldn't be yummy?!

INGREDIENTS

- **100g rolled oats**
- **8 tbsp cashew butter (or any nut butter of your choice)**
- **3 tbsp shelled hemp seeds or soya crispies (buy soya crispies online)**
- **8 tbsp vegan dark chocolate chips or cacao nibs**
- **4 tbsp syrup (eg maple or agave)**
- **1 tsp vanilla extract**
- **½ tsp ground cinnamon**
- **¼ tsp salt**

INSTRUCTIONS

1. Using a large mixing bowl, thoroughly combine all the ingredients until you get a smooth dough consistency. (If the mixture is sticking to your hands then add a few more oats until you get the desired texture. If the mixture gets too dry, just add a bit more nut butter.)

2. Line a square baking tin with greaseproof paper. It doesn't matter about the size too much as you can just sit the cookie dough mix inside without it needing to touch the sides.

3. Shape the dough so it's approximately 15cm x 15cm and around 2-3cm deep.

4. Press the mixture firmly and evenly into the tin and then place it in the fridge for a couple of hours to chill.

5. When ready cut it into 20 (approx.) little square bites.

6. Keep them in the fridge for up to 7 days in an airtight container or freeze them.

CHOCOLATE COCONUT BARS

LEVEL: EASY | PREP TIME: 10 MINUTES | COOK TIME: 1 HOUR | SERVES: 15

This is a much healthier (and of course, vegan) version of the classic bars and tastes even better than the original – coconut lovers rejoice!

INGREDIENTS

BARS
- **200g desiccated coconut**
- **200ml coconut milk (try to use equal quantities of the liquid and coconut cream layer at the top of the tin)**
- **4 tbsp syrup (eg maple or agave)**
- **2 tbsp coconut oil, melted**
- **2 tsp vanilla extract (optional)**

TOPPING
- **300g vegan chocolate of your choice (we used 70% cocoa solids), melted**
- **1½ tbsp coconut oil, melted**
- **¼ tsp salt**

INSTRUCTIONS

BARS
1. Place all the ingredients in a food processor and blend until combined. If you don't have a food processor, you can mix the ingredients up with a spoon then bring it together using your hands.
2. Shape the mixture into around 15 small bars. If you want them to be completely uniform then weigh them to 25g each approx.
3. Place them in the freezer on a lined tray to set for 30 minutes.

TOPPING
1. Melt the chocolate with the coconut oil using a double boiler/bain-marie (a glass or ceramic bowl that fits on a saucepan of simmering water but doesn't touch the bottom).
2. Pour the chocolate into a deep, narrow bowl or jug then dunk in each bar (using a fork) until fully covered.
3. Immediately make 3 marks on the top with the tip of a knife or spatula.
4. Place each bar onto a cooling rack with a lined tray underneath.
5. Pop the tray in the fridge for 30 minutes to chill.
6. Keep the bars in the fridge for up to 7 days in an airtight container or freeze them.